D0448220

"There is so much raw emotion in these pages—it is captivating, enthralling, and ultimately full of love and hope. Ben writes truth after truth about bringing a new child into this world—a complicated task always, regardless of personal situation. Once you read the first page you'll need to know how this particularly unique story ends—and Ben will beautifully tell you."

samantha bee

"I read this book once. Put it down on my bedside table and carried it around in my heart until I picked it up again and read for a second time…then a third. It's that good. It's that compelling. Mr. Barnz's heartrending honesty is about becoming yourself so your children can take their place in the world."

felicity huffman

"Ben Barnz's beautiful book is a moving reminder of the capacity of love. His account of how this one family was created is a roller coaster ride of emotions and a tidal wave of hope."

jesse tyler ferguson

"At once heart-warming and gut-wrenching, *We* had me on the edge of my seat. Ben Barnz brings his story to life with such honesty, vulnerability and humor, that I could not put it down. A must-read for anyone who has ever been a parent or had a parent. I did the same ugly-crying while reading as when I saw *Kramer v. Kramer* and *Terms of Endearment* for the first time. It will make you want to hug your people."

mark feuerstein

"This book grabs you like an infant's grasp on your finger—gentle and sweet, but there's no way you can let it go until it's done."

neil patrick harris

"Ben Barnz recounts his journey to fatherhood through the ups and downs of the complex adoption process. With precise emotional memory, Barnz unfolds this lump-in-your-throat, pit-in-your-stomach account of going from a 'me' to a 'we.' The boundless love, reverence and uncommon honesty he shows as he details his suspenseful and emotional path to parenthood will make you wonder if this page-turner of a story is, in fact, your story. Because it is. One way or another, it's all of our stories. I love this book."

dan bucatinsky

"Although *We* is a memoir, it reads like a novel in its scope, its momentum, its laser-eyed depictions of character, and—maybe most important —its depiction of the ways in which families, families of all kinds, are both powerful and precarious. Like a novel, *We* extends beyond its literal story, about two men adopting an infant, and speaks to us about elemental human desires, human will, and human fears. During these stormy political times, *We* is essential reading."

michael cunningham

"Ben Barnz wrote a book that proves definitively that the personal is political, we choose our families and that being yourself is the most sure fire path to nirvana. This story fills my heart with glad-ness even as it reminds me what a twisty turny road life is. You will want to be this writer's parent, spouse and child by the last page."

lena dunham

"Part memoir, part love letter, part haunting tale, *We* speaks in simple truths. What it means to be a father, a son, a partner, an adopted family. What it means to hold your baby girl knowing you may have to give her up. This gem of a first book burns deep with feeling, humor and the grace of salty tears. *We* is a work of shining honesty."

jodie foster

we

we

an adoption and a memoir

ben barnz

Wyatt-MacKenzie Publishing
DEADWOOD, OREGON

we
an adoption and a memoir
Ben Barnz

ISBN: 9781948018210, Hardcover
ISBN:9781948018227, Softcover
ISBN:9781948018234, eBook

Library Congress of Control Number: 2018948085

Wyatt-MacKenzie Publishing
DEADWOOD, OREGON

Published by Wyatt-MacKenzie Publishing
info@wyattmackenzie.com

for
my children who make me want to be better
and
my husband who loves me even when i am not

she asked
'you are in love
what does love look like?'
to which I replied
'like everything I've ever lost
come back to me.'

nayyirah waheed

Old paint on canvas, as it ages, sometimes becomes transparent. When that happens it is possible, in some pictures, to see the original lines; a tree will show through a woman's dress, a child makes way for a dog, a large boat is no longer on an open sea. That is called pentimento because the painter 'repented,' changed his mind. Perhaps it would be as well to say that the old conception, replaced by a later choice, is a way of seeing and then seeing again.

lillian hellman

f o r e w o r d

by
JESS CAGLE
Editor-in-Chief, PEOPLE

On Sept. 8, 2001, Ben Barnz and his husband Daniel are present at the birth of their adopted daughter, and bring her home the next day. Forty-eight hours later they wake in Los Angeles to the news of the 9/11 terrorist attacks. Another threat hits closer to home. As the new family is settling in, their daughter's biological father lays claim to her, and a shattering custody battle begins.

It's a hell of a story—eloquently, honestly and compellingly composed—but Ben Barnz's memoir is also the story of his own evolution growing up in New York City, coming out to his family, marrying his husband and starting a family only a few years after the idea of two married gay dads was unimaginable to many of us. With "We" Ben Barnz establishes himself as an important new voice speaking for Generation X—that sometimes cynical and relatively unexamined generation of latchkey kids and Grunge rock devotees born between the optimistic baby boomers and the entitled millenials. Ben came of age during the post Vietnam, post-Watergate and post-sexual revolution era of "malaise" when President Jimmy Carter bemoaned the nation's "crisis of confidence" during an energy crisis both literal and metaphorical. Then the world started spinning faster. Adapting to rapidly advancing technology, shifting cultural mores and America's increased vulnerability became a means of survival and a defining trait of Generation X.

For LGBTQ members of Generation X like Ben (and myself), advancements in civil rights happened so quickly we have sometimes struggled to fully embrace them. Born around the time of the Stonewall riots in 1969, many of us heard the word "gay" for the first time during Anita Bryant's virulently homophobic crusade during the 1970s. The AIDS crisis equated sexuality and death in our adolescent and young adult minds. Those wounds were still present when marriage equality became a reality. When Ben's family unit is threatened, he must fight not only his daughter's biological family, but also the demons that he realizes were never fully exorcised—the voices of fear, shame and guilt telling him that he's something of a fraud; that people like him do not deserve equal access to family.

Somewhere, Ben Barnz may be cringing at the idea that I've called him a voice of his generation. Indeed, Ben doesn't aspire to tell anyone's story but his own, and its power lies in his unvarnished honesty—the way he articulates his very complicated, very human feelings about himself, his parents, his husband and the bizarre events that unfold after they bring their baby home. To me the most striking and profound element of the book is something missing from it entirely. There is no villain to be vanquished here. Not because everyone behaves beautifully (in fact some of them behave terribly) but because Ben seeks to understand and, to a surprising degree, even embrace his tormenters. "It's important how things begin," he writes, and he never loses sight of that principle even as he's reminded time and again that the minutes and milestones of our lives are subject to forces and people unconcerned with our well-being. This is the inspiring, nail-biting story of the fighting, forgiveness and acceptance required to build a world of one's own.

1

I wanted you to hear this from me.

2

When I was one day old, my grandmother held me out of a hospital window five stories above Fifth Avenue. If she was over-excited, it was understandable. Her son, my uncle, had died of a heart attack a few months earlier and my arrival gave her a new grandson, a new life. My sisters, Julie, seven, and Andrea, four, were on the street below with my father, their eyes squinted, their little necks strained and tilted up, waiting to catch a glimpse of their new baby brother. Or at least that's how the story goes.

At my daughter's beginning, it is impossible not to think back on my own.

She is sound asleep in my arms, just several hours old.
"Who are you?" I ask.
The question hangs in the air.
The hospital room is dark, as the sun just recently set. The only light comes from the streetlamp outside. It is just the two of us.
"What is your story going to be?"

FROM THE DEPOSITION OF EMMA MURPHY
JANUARY 2002

Q: When did you first realize that you were pregnant with a child?

A: End of February.

Q: And did you do anything to confirm that you were pregnant?

A: I took a pregnancy test.

Q: A home-type test?

A: Yeah. And that's when I found out I was pregnant, beginning of March, late February.

Q: And between the time that you learned you were pregnant and when you saw him in March, did you attempt to call him [Liam]?

A: No.

Q: Is there any reason why you didn't attempt to call him?

A: I had planned on getting an abortion at that point.

Q: Did you change your mind—obviously—getting an abortion?

A: Right. I did not get an abortion.

Q: Why did you change your mind?

A: Because I was too far along to get a first trimester abortion.

Q: All right.

3

"Is this really happening?" I ask.

Daniel and I are at Good Samaritan Hospital in downtown Los Angeles and our child is being born across the hall. It is September 8th and Emma, our birthmother, is in labor. The hospital set up an additional birthing room for us and I am standing beside the warming table that has been turned on in anticipation of our baby's arrival. I wave my hand under the warmth of the red light, hot—cool—hot—cool.

I look into Daniel's almond-colored eyes and see apprehension wrestling with ecstasy. He is handsome. His hair is slightly grown out how I like it, allowing some curl to show. He could be a cousin of Mark Ruffalo. A friend once described me as the B-movie version of Keanu Reeves.

We arrived at the hospital eight hours ago. It is now just after four in the afternoon.

"We're going to be fathers," he says.

Fathers, I think and allow the word to bounce around inside of me.

I find myself in the hallway of the maternity ward before I

even realize my feet have moved. Daniel follows me and we begin to slide up and down the hall in our socks. We are the only people in the whole wing right now.

∼

Earlier in the morning we check in and are assigned a kind, no-nonsense nurse, who introduces herself as Mary. She hooks Emma up to various monitoring machines: one for her contractions, one for her heart and pulse rates, and another that keeps an eye on the baby. A woman down the hall is in the midst of what is a very difficult labor. Her screams ricochet all around us, loud and piercing.

"That will *not* be me," Emma states, definitively. She has extraordinary will power and I can't help but wonder if she will be able to make her labor brief and quiet.

We turn on a baseball game and hope the commentator and the crowds will drown out the screams.

Emma seems content for the moment, but after spending the past seven weeks with her, we have learned that she seldom shows her hand, and almost never asks for anything. We do, however, follow her lead and keep our own complex emotions in check. We are the excited, expectant parents but are cognizant that the woman going through the painful work is not in sync with our feelings.

We spend an hour or so playing Phase 10, a card game that helped occupy many of our previous days and nights together. Today Daniel and I cheat. We will not let Emma lose. Not today.

The woman's screams stop. Everything is still.

How many babies are born every second, I wonder.

Emma's monitor spikes, revealing a sharp contraction. Daniel and I hold our breath. Her hands drop onto her lap, displaying her cards. When the spike drops, she lifts her cards and we resume our game. She doesn't want us to ask if she is okay.

Twenty minutes later, a sharper spike arrives. Emma inhales sharply and I watch a single tear roll down her cheek.

She is absolutely alone.

Miles away from her family, friends, and any semblance of the life she knows. Or rather, the life she knew. She is having one of the most intimate, physically painful experiences one can have, with two men she didn't know existed sixty-five days ago.

Despite this shared event, our emotions are diametrically opposed.

Mary comes in to check on Emma. She is far enough along to get an epidural. We leave her alone for the procedure and when we return to her room fifteen minutes later, she asks us if we would "mind" if she rests for a while.

Daniel and I call our families and a few friends to give them an update and then, like men from days gone by, we spend a couple of hours in the hospital waiting room. Cast in the role of expectant straight father, kicked out of the delivery room and told to wait; only we are not those men and it is not the 1950s anymore. Yet here we are, alone, in a tiny room with uncomfortable chairs and a shared sandwich which we didn't want to eat in front of her. She can't eat anything until after the baby arrives.

At four o'clock, our obstetrician, Dr. Davis, arrives. We are on game fifty-five of Phase 10 and none of us is paying any attention. Daniel and I are sent out of the room so he can examine Emma, and that is where we are right now, in our socks, sliding up and down the hallway.

∾

Dr. Davis catches us mid-slide.

"Emma's fully dilated," he says, and smiles. He begins to explain to us what will happen next but I have a hard time hearing anything over the sound of my own fast-beating heart.

Focus, Ben.

"I'm going to have her start pushing," I hear him say, "but this can take a while so try to enjoy the calm before the storm." He starts to head back into her room and stops. "As you know, she's chosen not to see the baby, so we went ahead and set up a curtain for her. She told us, 'Ben and Daniel should see her first. They're her parents.'"

He steps back into her room and Daniel and I look at one another across the hall.

"I guess it *is* really happening," Daniel says.

∾

Thanksgiving, 1980. My parent's brownstone on the Upper West Side of Manhattan. I am fourteen years old, in eighth grade. I am skinny and awkward and my dark brown hair hangs razor straight. Thirty people sit around tables strewn with empty pie plates, half-drunk cups of coffee, and talk—there is always talking. I have carried my six-month-old nephew into the living room to give his mother a break. I am surprised by the intensity of love I feel for this small creature I barely know. He is so vulnerable. I lay him down on a soft blanket in a quiet corner and blow raspberry kisses on his stomach, which causes him to squeal with delight. His laugh is infectious.

I want to be a parent. I look up half-expecting to see someone talking to me. But before I am able to comprehend the joy that comes with this realization, that the voice is my own, my self-loathing and inner demons rear their ugly heads.

How can you be a father?

Fag.

It is the 1980s. Gay fathers are unheard of, even in New York City. It is statistically more likely I will die of AIDS than have a child.

~

"Ben!"

Daniel's voice brings me back to the present, back to the hospital, back to the life I forged for myself—

"She's here!"

—back to the birth of my child.

Emma's door flies open and Mary hurries across the hall with what looks like a bundle of white cloth in her arms. It has been twenty-two minutes since Dr. Davis told us to wait patiently because "this could take a while."

"Emma was remarkable," Mary says as we follow her into our room. "She pushed like a champ."

She gently lowers our baby girl onto the warming table.

Everything falls away. There is only you.

The warmth that radiates from the red light has an instantaneous effect on her tiny body. We witness her relax and then lengthen.

She opens herself up.

A piece of advice my mother gave me years earlier suddenly comes to mind:

It is important how things begin.

It is impossible not to marvel at this brand new life, this beginning. She is long and lovely. I silently count her fingers and toes and look up to see Daniel doing the same. Everything is in place. She has the smallest amount of blond fuzz on her head and her dark blue eyes blink continuously. She attempts to take in her new surroundings and I wonder what that must be like. To come from absolute darkness, silence and solitude into a world filled with light and sound and movement.

"I have to tell you," Mary says, breaking the silence, "I see a lot of babies and you've got an extremely alert one here."

An unearned sense of pride fills me when, as if on cue, our daughter expels the foulest black tar-looking sludge I have ever seen. It stops us cold.

"Perfectly normal," Mary reassures us, seeing our faces. "It's called meconium and she is doing exactly what she is meant to do. We want it out."

I watch as Mary scoops the sludge into a diaper with one hand, rolls it up and throws it away. Her other hand never leaves our baby's body. Her serenity blankets the room.

"We left the umbilical cord long so you guys could cut it," she tells us.

Daniel and I hesitate, moved by this gesture but uncertain how to proceed.

"There is no sensation in the cord, you won't hurt her," she says as she hands us a pair of scissors. "You can hold them together."

I look at Daniel and flash back to our commitment ceremony, his left hand in mine as I slipped a ring onto his finger.

He looks up and smiles.

I whisper, "Are you ready?"

Daniel rests his hand on mine and we snip the last remaining physical connection she has to her biological parent. The act feels symbolic, like we have executed a contract. We belong to one another now.

I look down at this new life under the glowing red light and for the first time I place my hand on her body. Her skin is ridiculously soft, like nothing I have ever felt.

"Hello," I say.

"Hello..." Daniel echoes. Her nose turns up slightly and I notice her coloring. She has a streak of red on each cheek, like a vertical brush stroke. Like permanent blush.

"Hi sweet girl," I murmur and wonder if she recognizes my voice. Daniel and I have been constant companions to Emma for the past two months.

Mary gently places our daughter on a scale. I flash to myself as a child looking up at my mother as she leans on the counter at our local butcher shop, checking the weight of a roast.

Emma's initial presence in Los Angeles altered my relationship with time; the appearance of our child seems to have pushed it somewhere else entirely.

The light outside shifts and the room becomes suffused with a golden glow.

"Seven pounds, nine ounces," Mary says, and brings me back to the present. She pulls out measuring tape and records her length. Twenty-two inches. She places her feet into an inkpad and gently presses each one on the hospital certificate: her first diploma, her first official document; all her information recorded except her name. We have not settled on a name.

A month earlier we finally narrowed our choices down to two. Daniel was adamant he wanted to see her before he decided and I agreed. We wanted to look into her eyes.

Your eyes are beautiful.

"You have all night to decide her name," Mary informs us as she places a small pink tub into the sink. "Bath time," she adds, with obvious joy in her voice.

Mary adjusts the water and uses the skin on the inside of her wrist to find an ideal temperature.

"Feel that," she says and places my wrist under the warm water. "That's a great temperature for her."

Daniel lifts our little girl from beneath the red light and cradles her, less than fifteen minutes old—new to the world, new to us, new to everything—and moves over to the tub. He beams. I have never seen him so content. For myself, the moment is incomprehensible. How is this our new reality? How is this child outside of her birthmother and a part of the world? How is this life our responsibility? We are both beaming now. My cheeks hurt.

"Make sure you keep a hand on the back of her neck. You are in for a treat."

Daniel lowers her into the tub and her eyes grow wide. I think I see a hint of a smile at the edges of her lips.

"Her first bath," Daniel says.

First everything.

I dip a washcloth into the water and gently run it across her bare chest, her arms, her legs, her neck. She allows this ritual to occur without fuss. Mary hands me a towel and Daniel lifts her out of the water and into my arms.

I hold you for the first time.

I breathe her in. I want to remember this moment for the rest of my life. She is not the only one born today. A long-held desire has been realized for me—I have become a we.

Mary demonstrates how to swaddle her so she is cocooned and secure.

At the door, she stops and turns: "Seems to me she's a pretty lucky little girl." And then she is gone.

In the quiet of the room, with the last bit of daylight crawling its way down the far wall and our child in my arms, time seems to stop. It feels as though we are utterly alone. The world outside doesn't exist.

"Daniel?" I whisper, asking a question which has no answer. He sits down next to me on the small couch in the darkening room.

It is overwhelming to hold a new life in my arms. We have been entrusted with her and the depth of that responsibility begins to sink in. I lean over and kiss Daniel's cheek and then I kiss her.

"I have to go home and get the adoption paperwork," Daniel says quietly. "I'll check in on Emma first. I'd ask if you were fine with me leaving but I know the answer."

I could not love him more—for knowing that, for knowing me.

I am thrilled to have some time alone with my daughter.

"Who are you?" I ask once Daniel is out of the room. "What's your story going to be?"

There is only the unknown ahead.

I wonder what my parents thought about in the first few moments of my life, what dreams and hopes they had for me. What it meant for them to have a son after two daughters, what it felt like to be responsible for three lives.

It is hard not to have them here. I rifle through our hospital bag for my cell phone. I need to hear their voices, to share with them the news of their fourth grandchild.

I dial automatically. Their number has not changed for thirty-five years.

My mother picks up the phone before the first ring is complete. "Well?"

"She's here," I say—and in that moment I know her name.

"Is she lovely? Wait. Irv!" she yells. "Pick up the phone!"

"She *is* lovely," I say and look down. She has fallen asleep.

"And how's Emma?"

"Resting. The labor lasted twenty-two minutes."

"Wow," I hear my mother say just as my father overlaps: "Hello?"

Hearing their voices is bittersweet. Lying in my arms is the continuation of our family history, another name added to our family tree. I love living in California and I love the life I have fashioned but the three-thousand mile distance, in this moment, feels crushing.

"Hi, Dad."

"Have you picked a name yet?" my dad asks.

"Not yet," I lie.

"Well, we can't wait to meet her," my mom says.

"...whatever her name is," my dad adds, laughing.

"We'll see you in a week," my mom adds. They had already bought tickets to come out and meet her.

"I love you," I whisper.

"We love you, too," they echo as we hang up.

For about an hour, I remain in this state of bliss when the door opens and the fluorescent light from the hallway spills into the darkened room. I instinctively move my hand to block the light from her eyes.

"I know her name," Daniel says, returning with the paperwork and dinner. He remains in the doorway, lit from behind.

"Me, too," I reply.

There is the briefest moment of concern. What happens if we chose different names?

"Should we say it at the same time?" I ask.

4

"Beautiful," Mary says an hour later. "Zelda is a strong name," she adds, as she leads us up to another floor where the three of us will spend the night. Emma has already been moved to another room and is asleep. Mary shows us how to prepare a bottle, and once again, leaves us alone. The exhaustion of the day crashes down on me. I feed Zelda who quickly falls back asleep. If we are spent I can only imagine what she must feel like. Daniel and I follow her lead and are asleep within minutes. I take the hospital bed and Daniel is on a rollaway. Throughout the night, nurses come in to check on Zelda and ask if we need anything. She eats every two hours. I feed Zelda. She sleeps. Daniel feeds her. We change her. The night passes. When the sun comes up Zelda is in my arms, wide-awake.

"Hi Zelda," I whisper.

"Morning daddy," Daniel says to me.

Our friend Ned arrives a couple of hours later. He is the first to hold her outside of Daniel and myself. Zelda's extended family grows. Our pediatrician arrives and runs a battery of tests. Before we leave, another friend, Laura, arrives and Zelda's family grows yet again. Before she can say goodbye a minor earthquake rocks the hospital. We huddle in the doorway with our arms wrapped around one another, Zelda tucked securely between us until it subsides.

"Welcome to the world," Laura whispers to Zelda, then leaves.

Mary places me in a wheelchair with Zelda in my arms.

"Hospital rules," she laughs, and wheels me to the back entrance.

Before she closes the car door she says, "I'm telling you, she's a very lucky little girl."

Then we drive away. The car ride home is silent. Zelda is asleep and neither of us wants to wake her up. I wonder if Daniel is experiencing similar emotions, something resembling wonder. How is it possible that we are able to leave a hospital with a human life and minimal instruction?

We pull up to our house, detach Zelda's car seat, and enter our home.

We stand side by side in our living room, frozen. Our overnight bag hangs from Daniel's shoulder along with the mail he grabbed on our way in. Zelda's car seat dangles in my right hand.

"Holy shit," Daniel says and drops the mail onto the coffee table.

"It's just us."

I expected the return home as freshly minted parents to feel significant but what I experience is smaller, more intimate. I see our house, our life, through a fresh pair of eyes. Daniel and I left as a couple and have returned a family.

"Should we show her around?" I ask, lifting her into my arms.

"Excellent idea," Daniel exclaims. He opens his arms wide and says, "Zelda, this is your living room," and laughs.

Life is good.

We bought the house two years ago. The neighborhood is called Hancock Park though really we live in "Hancock Park adjacent." Our house is a half block north of Melrose Avenue where Hancock Park technically ends and the three-thousand-square-foot houses become one thousand; I jokingly refer to it as The Wrong Side of the Tracks.

Our house has two bedrooms, one bath, and lots of light. In the backyard is a large fig tree, a small Meyer lemon tree, and a one-room bungalow, which Daniel uses as his office.

I follow Daniel as we tour Zelda around her new home. "Well," he says glancing around the living room, "this is a rocking chair," and I laugh. "What?" he asks. "She doesn't know what a rocking chair is."

Everything is new.

The chair sits by the fireplace, upholstered with a rich, golden stripe fabric. I have always loved the chair but even more so since we placed it by the window. I point out the first "real" piece of art we bought, which consists of three small books fired in clay and overlaid with a photo of an old woman. The piece is delicate and haunting and reminds me of Lillian Hellman's *Pentimento*—always something hidden and unseen.

We walk into our bedroom where the walls are painted a soft, grassy green. A pair of long, heavy curtains conceals a window that looks out onto our side yard. I am excited to point out her bed: the Co-Sleeper is a three-sided crib that attaches directly to our bed.

In the kitchen we point out all the baby bottles that line the window ledge above the sink.

Then we make our way down the hallway lined with old family photos. "These are your grandparents," I show Zelda, "and these are your cousins."

We tell her that the den will be her room one day, though for now it is our TV room. There is a large white couch and just yesterday we added a glider chair for feedings. We open the set of French doors that lead outside. The fresh air feels good. The covered patio has a round wooden dining table. "That's a fig tree," Daniel points out as he steps into the yard. "And way back there is a Meyer lemon tree." Daniel starts to walk out to his office, but as I step into the backyard the bright sun causes Zelda to tuck her little head into the crook of my elbow. I melt. I kiss her head and turn back to the house. "We'll show you the yard later," I say, back in the safety of the shade. "We have nothing but time."

I want so much for her. I want to teach her, guide her—help her become a life to be reckoned with.

We give her a bath. Daniel places the plastic bathtub from the hospital into our kitchen sink. I adjust the water temperature with the back of my wrist.

Daniel keeps his hand on the back of her neck and lowers her into the water while I take a washcloth and wipe down her skin. Her body relaxes in the warmth of the water. I can see her let go. Daniel lifts her up and I wrap her in a towel that dwarfs her and together we walk into our bedroom, neither of us wanting to leave the other's side. Or hers.

He hands me a t-shirt and a diaper.

"We make a good team," I say.

"We do," he says and gives her belly a kiss.

"I'll make a bottle," I tell Daniel as he takes Zelda into the den, where I hear him ask if she would like to read a book. This bliss is like nothing I have ever experienced.

I start down the hall with her first homemade bottle when the phone rings. The sound invades our sanctuary.

"Hello?"

"Welcome home."

It takes me a moment to place Jonathan Ross's voice. He is our adoption lawyer.

"Why thank you. Glad to be home."

"Good. Hope you three are doing well. The first few weeks can be a lot."

I am glad we hired him. He is kind.

"So, I need to let you know that I got a call from Liam's sister, Melissa, yesterday."

Liam is Zelda's biological father.

My mouth goes dry.

I make my way into the den as I listen to Jonathan shuffle some papers on his desk.

"What?" Daniel asks when he sees my face.

"Liam's sister called Jonathan," I say. I do nothing to hide the anxiety in my voice.

"I sent you a letter," I hear Jonathan say. "I know this is not easy to hear but trust me more often than not these calls are just chatter. A family member finds out at the last minute and makes some noise."

I turn around and walk into the living room where I flip through the mail that we ignored when we first got home. Near the bottom of the pile I find the letter.

"Liam told Emma that adoption was the best choice," I say. "I don't understand what's happening."

Back in the den, I open the letter and then hand it to Daniel, who still holds Zelda in his lap. I clench her bottle in my hand.

"Are you there?" Jonathan asks.

"Yes. Sorry. We have the letter."

"Let's see what happens, but honestly, just enjoy your daughter and we will see where this goes. As I said, more often than not it is nothing."

"Um," I mutter. "Sure. Bye." I hang up the phone.

Daniel gets up from the glider so we can sit together on the couch. I take Zelda and feed her while Daniel reads the letter aloud:

Gentlemen:

I want to inform you that I received an email today from Melissa Richards who claims to be Liam Flynn's sister. I had a telephone conversation with her later in the day. Ms. Richards indicates that Liam will not agree to "turn over" his paternity rights. She stated, "We would like all the information possible so that he has an opportunity to exercise his paternal rights. Please help us in regards to this case." I informed her in my telephone conversation with her that I could not speak to her; I could only speak to Liam. I told her that I would be willing to talk to him and, in fact, had already spoken to him previous to my conversation with her. I advised her that I had never heard back from him after that call.

Ms. Richards persisted in attempting to elicit information and to inform me that Liam was opposed to the adoption. I have not heard from Liam....

"I'm going to finish feeding her in the living room," I manage to get out with what little breath is in my body. I don't want to hear anymore. I don't want to finish the letter. Zelda needs attending to and I am close to throwing up.

I hurry out of the den—the room we just finished saying would one day be hers. Now I am not so sure.

Zelda is asleep in my arms when Daniel joins me on the couch in the living room.

"I have to believe that Jonathan knows what he is talking about," Daniel says almost inaudibly.

"Yes," I reply. "He's been doing this for years."

"That's right," he adds and stands up. "I need to sleep. I'm exhausted and I don't think clearly when I'm like this."

We place Zelda in her co-sleeper and Daniel and I climb into bed. It is just after 9 PM.

"We will figure this out," he whispers before he kisses me goodnight, places his second pillow over his head, and falls asleep.

I lay motionless between the two human beings I love most in the world, knowing that I should follow suit, that I must get some rest, that things won't look so bleak in the morning. But a battle has begun to rage within me between the love I feel for Zelda and the terror of losing her. I have been waiting for her since I was a teenager. Perhaps Jonathan is right and this is just noise. I have to believe that, otherwise I don't know how to face tomorrow. I force my mind to concentrate on the fact that my long-held dream has become a reality.

Eventually I drift off.

When my eyes pop open in the middle of the night, I am thrilled to realize that my first thought is of my daughter and not the potential threat of losing her. She is asleep beside me and the light from the moon creeps through our curtains and makes me wonder if we should get blackout shades. Her diaper is comically full and her soft blue t-shirt has moved up to reveal her perfect little belly.

I am frightened by how protective I feel toward her after only two days. Years later, a friend will tell me that having her first child "burst her heart wide open." I love Daniel with all my heart, but I would kill for Zelda.

I cannot help but laugh at how fast our home has been transformed by this creature. There is no question now that a baby lives within these walls. The Baby Bjorn hangs, blue and twisted, on the back handle of our bedroom door. Two days ago, our dresser was a place to store our wallet and keys. A photo of Daniel and me holding a friend's Oscar sat beside another one of us hiking in Joshua Tree. All of that is gone now. Zelda's changing pad leaves just enough room for her diapers, wipes, and a stack of tiny clothes. On the front porch, a stroller sits and the drying rack next to the kitchen sink is full of empty bottles.

Zelda's needs spill over into every nook and cranny of our home and I love it. I relish it. Being Jewish and sporadically superstitious, we had decided not to unpack any baby paraphernalia until after she was born. God might smite our certitude.

Now I want to curse that same God. We never counted our blessings in advance, but Liam's sister still called.

Friends come to meet Zelda, bearing food and gifts. Everything I used to do falls away. We manage to feed ourselves here and there, but it seems our days of home-cooked meals are on hold indefinitely.

I am in a state of intoxicated bliss.

By the end of the day we have heard nothing from Jonathan.

"No news is good news, right?" I ask Daniel as he tiptoes out of our bedroom after putting Zelda down for the night.

"Absolutely," he says. He reaches into the cabinet and pulls out a bottle of scotch. "Come sit with me?" He grabs two glasses and some ice and heads outside. I start to follow him but stop when I glance down at Jonathan's letter lying on the kitchen counter. The last line leaps out at me:

I don't anticipate this to be anything other than the norm.

Nothing feels normal and I find myself angry with Jonathan for appearing so blasé. Then my anger turns to Liam's sister, this stranger who I didn't even know existed, who has now brought fear and uncertainty into our lives.

"Ben?" I hear Daniel call. "Come outside."

Today there was no news from Jonathan, making it a good day. Perhaps it *is* just noise.

I peek in on Zelda who is fast asleep before I join Daniel outside. He sits at the table under the clear night sky and hands me a drink.

Daniel raises his glass, "To fatherhood."

5

My eyes snap open.

Fuck.

The sunlight has barely made its way into our room. I fling myself out of bed and grab the phone in the kitchen before it's able to ring a second time. I am sure it is Jonathan with more bad news, and I do nothing to hide my irritation.

"Hello?" My voice is hard and cold.

"Ben, turn on your television."

Not Jonathan.

It is Lizz, one of my oldest friends. We met the first day of our sophomore year at The Bronx High School of Science, in 1981. We both grew up in Manhattan and were inseparable from the moment we met. Lizz moved to Los Angeles several years after me and is calling from the East Coast where she is covering the Toronto Film Festival for *People Magazine*.

The clock on the kitchen wall says it is just before six in the morning. It can never be good news when someone calls so early.

"Ben," she says again, "turn on your TV." Her usually animated voice is shaking.

"What?"

"Ben," she says and slows down her words. "I need you to walk to your den and turn on the television."

Not awake enough to argue, I obey. It doesn't occur to me to wonder why she hasn't asked after Zelda.

I dig the remote control out from between the cushions of the couch and turn on the TV. Immediately, I am bombarded with incomprehensible images. Smoke billows out of the Twin Towers and it looks as if people are leaping from windows that should not be open.

"Ben—" Lizz begins, but there is nothing to say.

It is September 11, 2001.

Daniel is asleep and I hate that I have to bring him into this day.

"It's not Jonathan," I whisper as his eyes pop open. "But I need you to come with me." He stumbles half asleep into the den.

We sit and watch the unfathomable unfold. I call my family, who all live on Manhattan's Upper West Side. The unsteadiness I hear in their tried and true New Yorker voices frightens me. It takes Daniel over an hour to reach his two sisters who work downtown.

Within the hour, our doorbell starts to ring and friends show up, unannounced, anxious and confused. The need to be together is immediate and intense. I find myself grateful that our house is the home to which people want to come. I sit in the back of our den with Zelda in my lap and watch everyone watch the television. It is a dreadful loop. The Chyron reads: *America Attacked*.

Everything is speculation, but the terror is real.

It is impossible not to feel that everything is falling down around me. Was it really just last night that Daniel and I decided not to tell anyone about Liam's sister? There is nothing to say now anyway, and I couldn't stand seeing my own anxiety reflected back at me—or worse, pity. Now everyone is living a collective nightmare, and anxiety is everywhere. Where does our personal nightmare fit?

Despite this terrorist attack in my parent's backyard, I know they would never for a moment consider leaving their beloved city. That unsettles me even more.

~

My parents moved to Manhattan in 1959. My mother Elaine declares it to be the "greatest city in the world," and that mantra has informed her whole life.

She was pregnant with my oldest sister, Julie, when they moved into the Park West Village apartment complex on 96th Street and Columbus Avenue. My mother insists they chose the neighborhood and the apartment because, "they were brand new and didn't smell like shit."

When I turned two, they moved my sisters and me into a brownstone on 94th Street between Central Park West and Columbus Avenue. Blessed with excellent housing karma, and the fact that at that time the Upper West Side was extremely under-developed, they bought it for next to nothing. We lived in the bottom three floors and my parents wisely designed four rentals on the top two floors that eventually paid off their mortgage. The high-ceiling living room had three soaring arched glass windows and art all over the walls, including an architectural rendering of the Paris Opera House. The room faced our quiet tree-lined street. The open dining room and kitchen had a twelve-foot-long counter and two glass doors; the space was flooded with light. In the backyard, we rode bikes, played with our black Labrador, Jingles, buried our hamster, and celebrated my secular Bar Mitzvah. A wide wooden flight of stairs led down to all the bedrooms, my parents' room was strategically next to the front door; there could never be any sneaking in after curfew. A bright red flight of stairs led down to the basement where we watched television and hosted Halloween parties, where we dunked for apples and tried to catch marshmallows on a string. In a far back corner, a storage room housed an old water heater, when it turned on, it made a startling, deafening rumble that terrified me as a child.

~

The TV network's loop of the plane and its thundering roar heading toward the Towers brings me back to our den. Feeling fortunate to have Zelda as a distraction, I remove myself from the endless repetition of destruction on the television and head into the kitchen to make her a bottle.

"Still no news from Jonathan," Daniel says.

I appreciate his ability to find the sliver of light in a day full of darkness.

"True. Can you hold her a minute so I can make a bottle?"

"Of course," he says, happy for the diversion.

"I want her back though."

He carefully pours himself a cup of tea while I make a bottle; each of us lost in our own thoughts.

I wonder if today's events will influence Liam's decision to contest the adoption. His silence led us to believe he was not going to object to the adoption. And why is his sister calling and not Liam himself? Is she allowed to insert herself into this situation? It's hard not to feel as if we should have asked Emma more questions about Liam. We never bothered to learn much about him. Her antagonism toward Liam was apparent; Daniel and I chose to respect that. We learned virtually nothing, except that he is tall and, according to Emma, "kind of cute."

Now I hate this person.

Zelda greedily latches onto the bottle as I take her back from Daniel, who reluctantly gives her up.

A choked gasp comes from someone in the den. There is repeated footage of the buildings collapsing and thick, gray dust covering the streets and the people on those streets. I swallow the urge to scream at the top of my lungs.

Darkness is all around.

"I need to hold her," Daniel says and takes Zelda from my arms without waiting for a response. Feeling exposed and alone, I smile. It's a cheap trick I learned from someone, though I can't recall from whom. When I feel deflated or want to stop myself from spinning into darkness, I literally force myself to smile. My mind gets tricked into a feeling of positivity. Somehow, it works. I look around the room with my smile and take in my friends, my Los Angeles family, and I find a ray of hope. Daniel and I have managed to create a hub and I silently thank my mother for teaching me how to do that.

From my mother, Elaine, I inherited my fervent nurturing instinct, a deep (and not altogether healthy) sense of co-dependence, as well as the ability to read people and situations instantly. Like my mother, I get a great deal of pleasure taking care of those closest to me.

My mother was raised in Orange, New Jersey, or what she likes to refer to as "Plain Orange," or the "wrong side of Orange." She worshipped her mother, Rose, who lived to make others happy and made a remarkable chocolate chip cookie. My mother's father, Louis, was a lawyer as well as a shyster who held onto his magnificent head of white hair until he passed away at eighty-six. My mother's older brother, Bobby, died of a heart attack at the age of thirty-nine. I was born three months later.

Her brother's early death prompted my mother to "treat every day as though it is not only my last but everyone else's around me," she told me one day over margaritas during a family vacation in Mexico. "Which is why you shouldn't get mad about petty things and most things are really very petty."

Seven years after her brother died, Rose died of angina. At the time, I was seven years old and was convinced that angina had something to do with her vagina, but I was too afraid (and embarrassed) to ask how her vagina could kill her. Her mother's death cemented my mother's need to keep those she loves as close as possible and show them her love on a daily basis.

I consider calling my parents again just to hear their voices, but I decide to leave them alone. They don't need to worry about my concerns for them or my concern for our world. Also, Zelda needs a nap.

I am telling you now, always call. I will always want to hear from you.

The only sound in the den comes from the television. The images are so relentlessly devastating that there are stretches when even the commentators are silent; what is there to say? I imagine their silence mirrors households across the country, throughout the world. It certainly is the case in our den where everyone attempts to process the horror.

The phone rings and Daniel and I lock eyes. He gets up and walks down the hall. I hold Zelda in my arms and watch him turn into the kitchen in order to answer the phone. I wait for his expression to tell me it is Jonathan and Liam has contacted him.

"It's your dad," he says as he steps into the hall.

He hands me the phone and smiles. Relief. I pass him Zelda.

"Are you okay?"

"We're okay," my dad says, though I can hear his anxiety, repressed.

"Can I do anything for you?"

"No. We are fine." Repress. "We won't be able to come out next week for obvious reasons." Repress. "But we will come out the following week. Nothing will keep us from meeting our newest granddaughter."

"Of course," I say and add my own lie. "And we are fine, too." Repress. We haven't told them about Liam or his sister's letter.

We are all fine. Everyone is fine.

There are times when a lie is better.

"She can't wait to meet you. She is delicious."

The doorbell rings and I watch Daniel walk toward the front of the house.

"Very good," my father says, "we'll speak later."

"I love you," I say and hear him echo the sentiment before he hangs up.

From my father, Irv (a man who was mistaken for Woody Allen more than once when he was in his forties), I inherited the ability to speak to strangers. This is a talent he enjoys and I find necessary. I have also inherited his ability to lash out (though that might be the Scorpio in me), an inquisitive mind, a barrel-chested build, and an almost compulsive need for some amount of daily solitude.

The youngest of five children, my father was raised on the west side of Chicago. The youngest of five by nine years, his closest sibling volunteered to fight in World War II, essentially leaving my dad an only child, who grew into a man most at ease on his own.

"I ordered some pizza," Daniel says after I hang up the phone. He balances Zelda, two pizza boxes and a salad.

I find myself wrestling with the fact that despite today's tragic events, life goes on. It has to. Pizza gets made. People need to eat. The sun will set and then rise on a new day. Zelda will need to be changed. I will need to sleep. I can't help but worry about the world Zelda will be raised in. Today's events changed it forever.

While Daniel carries plates and food into the den, I pause in front of the photos in the hallway. Does every generation think their time was simpler? I stare at a favorite picture of mine, which my father must have taken. It shows my sisters and me with my mother in Paris. I am wearing a striped fisherman's shirt, both of my sisters have long pigtails and my mother looks much more stylish then I remember in a pair of large black sunglasses. It's impossible, with all that is going on, not to think about my nuclear family.

Every day of first grade my father walked me to school with our black Labrador in tow. This was unusual; most of my friends had to find their own way to school.

I was eleven years old when we spent August in a farmhouse in the south of France. I had my own room for the first time. On a daily basis my father killed scorpions that found their way into the bathtub. We had non-stop visitors despite the remoteness of the house on the hill, and my sisters discovered a payphone in the center of town that allowed them to call their boyfriends in the United States for free.

Every day of high school my mother made me lunch. It was in the refrigerator each morning, packed and waiting. My envious friends would always try to steal parts of it.

Every evening we had dinner together. We sat around the black oval dining table and ate a homemade meal. We discussed our days; I spat my vegetables into my napkin until I was in my teens.

Mainly I remember that they were always there. They were present.

They were there in Paris when I fell off a fence and got a concussion. My mother rushed me to a hospital where I was given a large bowl of coffee—basically warm milk, a splash of coffee and tons of sugar. I was three. This is my first memory.

They were there when I was seven and spending August on Fire Island, a sliver of beach outside New York City with no cars and endless wooden boardwalks. I was excited to show off my newfound bicycle riding skills to visiting friends, but instead found myself flying off the boardwalk. I landed in the thorny brush. Terrified and humiliated, I was lifted, bloodied and crying, into my father's arms.

At our commitment ceremony in their backyard in Southampton, New York, they spoke during our ceremony and sung their toast at the reception. Both of my sisters were married in the same place.

Tradition is my family's religion.

Reentering the den, I am moved by a fleeting sense of peace, or perhaps clarity; in spite of the day's events and the threat of Liam and all the uncertainty that surrounds us, I find solace knowing I am reconciled with my past. I have begun to build my own lore and my own traditions. Zelda is an essential part of that.

It has been a draining day. No one at our house had anyone directly affected by the day's atrocities, though I will later discover that my first boyfriend, Steven, escaped from one of towers, and that a friend's mother was in one of the planes which crashed. By six o'clock everyone has left our house.

Three days ago our daughter was born and the world seemed right. Two days later her biological father's sister called and up-ended our lives. Today, terror went global; everything has been shaken to its core and I find myself searching for something solid to grasp hold of.

6

The following morning I stand alone at our dining room table and stare down at the front page of *The New York Times*: U.S. AT-TACKED: HIGHJACKED JETS DESTROY TWIN TOWERS. The phone rings and I know what is coming because the world is falling apart.

"Hello?" I answer curtly.

"Ben?"

I am right. The world is falling apart. It is Jonathan Ross, and his gentle tone irritates me.

Let's get through this, I think. None of this is Jonathan's fault. He is just the messenger. I feel sweat break out along my hairline.

"Liam is going to contest the adoption."

Even though I knew it was coming the room goes soft around the edges. For a moment the only thing in focus is a neatly folded dishtowel that rests on the wooden island in the middle of our kitchen. There is a distinct taste of metal in my mouth and I lean against the counter so I won't fall down. I can't think of anything to say.

I know I ought to speak, defend, yell, say something. But I can't find my voice.

Why am I always the one awake to answer these calls?

"Ben?" Jonathan's voice breaks the silence.

I need Daniel, I think.

"Hold on," I say.

I make my way into our room and sit on the edge of our bed. Once again, I have to wake Daniel from his dreams into a nightmare. Yesterday it was 9/11. Today is closer to home.

"Daniel?"

His eyes flutter open as he gets his bearings. He looks drawn and I wonder for a split second if I should have just let him sleep. He sits up as soon as he sees my face.

"He's contesting the adoption." I don't even want to say his name and I hate that I have to say it so close to Zelda's ears.

Daniel's eyes dart over to Zelda.

"Over my dead fucking body," he says and gets out of bed.

With the phone pressed up against our ears, Daniel and I stand in the kitchen and listen to Jonathan tell us "not to worry too much about it right now." He tells us that we "need to take this one day at a time" and "it still all might go away."

My anger swells.

"Liam may not even follow through with his threat."

"I need to call you back," I say.

"That's fine. But you should call Emma," Jonathan says, before I hang up.

Daniel looks at me, confused.

"I couldn't listen to him hypothesize anymore."

Rage courses through me while Jonathan's voice plays on a loop inside my head: Liam is contesting the adoption. Liam is contesting the adoption. Liam is contesting the adoption. I leave the kitchen and pace the living room.

Daniel gives me space.

The thing—the person—the job I have wanted most in the world might be taken away from me and I want to hurt something, someone. I want to cause pain.

"What are we going to do?" I hate the whine I hear in my voice.

Daniel is on the couch. His lips draw together in a tight line as he formulates a plan. I just react.

"There's no way he will win this," he says. His calm irritates me. "We have Emma on our side." He pulls me down next to him.

"I want your confidence," I say.

"I have it today. You will have it tomorrow."

He goes to get dressed. Left alone I don't know what to do with myself. A basket of clean laundry sits in the living room. I drag the basket toward me.

Fold. Don't think. Fold.

"Can he just *do* this?"

Daniel's harsh tone startles me. "Who would do such a thing?"

"An asshole. That's who."

"What else did Jonathan say?"

"I told you everything he said. Which was basically nothing."

"Don't do that, Ben. I need to know everything he said." His tone is cold, his words clipped.

Rage grows inside me; because he stands in front of me, he will bear the brunt of my fury.

"Don't patronize me. Don't. I told you everything he told me." I am standing now, clenching Zelda's tiny t-shirt in my hand. "You were on the call for most of it." I almost trip over the laundry basket and kick it instead.

We both stand looking at one another, daring the other to speak. The air feels combustible. Daniel must sense this, too, because he starts to approach me, then stops. Neither of us wants comfort right now. We want to be angry.

Outside, a car horn blares.

Zelda wakes up and needs to be changed. Daniel has to write. We have no food in the house. I take Zelda to the market.

Life goes on. The sun will set.

There are brief moments throughout the morning when I forget about Liam, about Jonathan's call, about 9/11; then they flood back in. I can't help but wonder if this is the new normal.

Returning home, I unpack the groceries, feed Zelda, read her a book, and put her down for a nap.

Daniel comes in from his office for lunch.

"Have you called Emma?" he asks.

"Why do I always have to be the one to make these calls?"

The statement comes out more harshly than I intended. Daniel lets it slide.

"I'll do it," he says. "But I need to eat something first."

"No. It's fine," I tell him, "Eat. I want to call her."

Taking care of Emma was always more my responsibility. We've spent more time together since she has been here in Los Angeles. And I am just better on the phone than Daniel. Though none of that particularly matters; this is a dreadful call to make.

"What if her fear gets the better of her?" I ask and reach for the phone. "What if she sides with him just to make this end? To make it all go away."

"She won't," Daniel says.

He sounds deflated. It breaks my heart but I can't help myself.

"You don't know that."

"You're right, I don't."

Please don't leave it at that, I think.

"But I don't *see* her saying that," he adds.

Thank you.

I take the phone with me into the living room and sit down on the couch. I imagine Emma sitting on her couch: the television blasting whatever football game is on at the moment. She has been staying at the Park LaBrea apartments, a gated community centrally located in Los Angeles. Though it's walking distance from a Kmart and a supermarket she has never gone out on her own. She has been there since she arrived two months ago.

She answers. I tell her the little we know.

"Why is he doing this?" she asks when I am done. Her voice cracks.

"Jonathan says it's probably just noise. That most likely nothing will come of it." I want to believe this. Perhaps it's true.

"I really don't want my parents to find out."

This frightens her more than anything and I have no idea how to respond. I wish I could promise her that they won't, that the choices she has made are hers to tell, but I can't. Despite her claim that she is close with her family, she has kept her pregnancy a secret. But now the number of people who know about her pregnancy has grown and she might not be able to control it.

"Will he tell them?" she asks. Panic has crept into her voice. "Should I call him? Shit. Do you think he is going to tell them?"

I find myself irrationally irritated by her stream of questions and immediately hate myself for it. I suffer from a need to fix things for others and my inability to fix this makes me feel powerless. Emma has done everything to care for Zelda and herself and she has every right to be upset. There is a penetrating silence that neither of us attempts to fill. We are out of our element, unmoored and uncertain how to move ahead.

"You're her parents," Emma says.

A vein in my neck begins to pulse.

"You're Zelda's parents," she says again.

FROM THE DEPOSITION OF EMMA MURPHY
JANUARY 2002

Q: Did you have a particular reason or desire to place the child in California?

A: I just—I didn't want to give birth in Stillwater, or I didn't want to—for anyone to know I was pregnant.

Q: So you wanted to be out of Minnesota?

A: Yeah.

Q: But California had no special circumstances over New York or North Carolina?

A: No.

Q: You spoke with another agency prior to speaking with Jonathan Ross, is that correct?

A: Yes.

Q: When is the first time you spoke with Jonathan Ross?

A: I believe I called him July 5th because I was supposed to leave for California July 7th through the other adoption agency, and I hadn't spoken with them. I was seven and a half months pregnant, and I still was in Stillwater, and they weren't going to move me out of Stillwater, and they had said they were going to.

Q: How long after you spoke to Jonathan Ross did he introduce you to Daniel and Ben?

A: The same day, actually.

Q: Did you tell anyone in your family about your pregnancy?

A: Just my sister.

Q: Did your sister give you any advice with regard to what you should do with respect to Liam?

A: No. She never really liked Liam too much. So she—she didn't even want me to tell him at all actually.

Q: Between your talk with Liam and prior to leaving for California did you have any contact of any kind with Liam?

A: I spoke with him twice more on the phone, and once where I work.

Q: Do you recall the substance of that conversation?

A: Yes. That one was the first time that he actually said that adoption seemed to be the best thing for me to do.

Q: And did he say anything to you in that conversation other than adoption may be the best thing?

A: Yes. He asked if I had gone to a doctor. He asked if I had considered raising the child myself. And that was about it. And then he called me names.

Q: The way you say that I trust that wasn't nice names?

A: No, it wasn't.

7

July 5, 2000. Two months before Zelda's birth and forty-five minutes before I'll speak with Emma for the first time. Daniel is in the middle of his midday nap when the phone rings.

"Daniel?

"No. It's Ben."

"It's Jonathan Ross. Are you ready?" he asks. He is never one for small talk.

"Sure."

"Her name is E-"

"Oh...no...wait! I don't have a pen." I am frantic.

"So you weren't ready?"

Was that a test? Did I just fail? Does he now think me unfit to parent?

I just didn't have a pen, I want to say. I *am* ready to parent. I have been ready since I was fourteen. I grab a pen from a kitchen drawer.

"I'm ready," I say, triumphant.

"Her name is Emma. She's due in September."

I scribble down her name and phone number and underline two months.

"She's waiting for your call. Good luck."

This is it. The illusion of a birthmother becomes a reality with a thirty-second phone call, a name, and a number. I feel like I am on speed. Her name stares back up at me. Two-months pulsates on the page. I underline it again so hard that I tear through the piece of paper.

I head into our bedroom and stand over Daniel. I fantasize about grabbing the other pillow and sticking it under my t-shirt but I can't contain my excitement anymore so I just grab his pillow—

"We might be pregnant!"

He is awake in an instant.

"What?"

"Her name is Emma."

"Wait...what?"

"Jonathan called."

"When?" he asks, bounding out of bed.

"Just now," I say as I follow him into the bathroom. He splashes water on his face.

We make our way into the kitchen as he presses me for more information I don't have. I show him the piece of paper on the kitchen island. All it has on it is her name, number, and the fact that we could be parents before Labor Day.

"You should speak with her," he suggests, finding a yellow legal pad and two pens. "You're better on the phone."

"True enough," I respond.

He smiles, "Fine, but you don't have to agree so quickly."

It doesn't even occur to us to wait. We know we are not the only potential adoptive family Jonathan will introduce her to and we want to get to her first.

We establish rules for the call: Daniel can listen—from a distance—and if there is something he feels he must communicate with me, he can write it down. But then he has to go away again. I don't want him hovering.

Daniel pours himself a cup of coffee and takes it outside, where I now watch him pace around the patio. He looks so cute in his shorts, his hair curling in the humid July air. He clutches a yellow legal pad to his chest.

The phone sits before me. All I need to do is reach down and pick it up.

"Wait," he yells and runs into the den. I hear him rifling

through some papers. I poke my head down the hallway just as he walks toward me with a piece of paper in his hand. Two months earlier, Jonathan Ross walked us through a sample conversation with a prospective birthmother designed to gather information about her and her situation. He stressed that the call must feel spontaneous and unrehearsed, that we had to be "present."

Of course we immediately went home and wrote ourselves a script.

> 1. Thank you for calling. We really want to adopt. I guess this is an open adoption, please ask us anything.
>
> 2. You know what, let me tell you about me.
>
> 3. Tell her about activities you do (in order to learn more about her and —
>
> 4. Her activities: (underline things you have in common)
>
> 5. Let me tell you about Daniel. (Give information about Daniel to get information about the birthfather)
>
> 6. This child will be so loved.
>
> 6. Tell her about our families and how happy they are that we are starting a family.
>
> 7. Tell me about your family, what are their thoughts about all this?
>
> 8. Can I send you an album of photos we put together, would it be all right to send it overnight?
>
> 9. Thank you so much!

I could simulate spontaneity but I didn't want to forget any crucial information.

"Good luck," Daniel says and makes his way back outside. "You'll be great," he shouts over his shoulder.

I glance over our script. Notes will be crucial; Daniel will want every detail.

"Wait!" Daniel shouts again and comes into the kitchen. He fills a glass of water, places it in front of me.

He smiles at me before disappearing onto the patio.

I take a deep breath to steady my nerves and then I dial her number.

"Emma?"

"Yes."

"Hi, this is Ben. Jonathan Ross gave us your number."

"Oh, hi." There is a hint of a Midwestern accent.

"Let me start," I say, "by just telling you how much we have always wanted a child and thank you for considering us."

She doesn't respond so I push forward. We are both nervous.

"I guess this is an open adoption, so please feel free to ask me anything you want."

"Okay."

Jonathan suggested that in order to get information, we must give information. I tell her I was born and raised in New York City but have been living in Los Angeles for years. I tell her about my two older sisters and how they both continue to live in Manhattan. I tell her my parents still live in the same house where we all grew up. I pace around the kitchen island in circles.

She tells me that she is twenty-three and has two sisters; she is the oldest. She tells me she lives on her own but also lives close to her family. Only her middle sister knows about her pregnancy.

Daniel ducks into the den.

She tells me she is a waitress.

"I waited tables too," I laugh. "I thought I was fantastic."

"Thought?" she asks.

"Yeah," I continue, as I hear Daniel making his way down the hall. What is he doing? "After I was fired from my third restaurant I realized I wasn't."

Her laugh is generous. There is a pause.

"I need to leave town as soon as possible," she says. "I'm starting to show."

I scribble down: heavy?!?

I can't find any other explanation for why a woman who is seven months pregnant to only just begin to show.

"That's no problem," I tell her. "We can get you out here quickly."

A sound of ripping paper comes from the hallway and I turn around to see Daniel dropping a piece of yellow paper onto the kitchen island:

YOU ARE GIVING US <u>SUCH</u> A GIFT!

His words cover the entire page.

He darts back outside. For a split second, I think about how difficult it would be for me *not* to be on this call.

Shit.

There is silence on the phone. Emma and I had been on a roll and I am thrown. I don't think it is the time to say this but I have to do something to recover, so I read Daniel's words aloud:

"You are giving us such a gift!"

She doesn't respond. She hasn't given you anything yet, idiot!

I stick my head down the hall. Daniel has a questioning smile on his face. I shake my head and shoo him away with my hand.

Daniel can only hear one side of the conversation. I can handle this.

Give to get.

"Do you have any pets?" I ask. People love to talk about their animals, so my fingers are crossed. "We have a big dog named Sadie."

"I have three cats," she says.

Bingo.

"I love cats," I lie. I am more of a dog person.

"I need them to come with me."

I scribble down: *must fly cats = 3*

"What are their names?"

"Nick, Kevin and A.J.," she laughs apologetically, "I named them after The Backstreet Boys."

"They have some good songs," I lie again. I couldn't name one of their songs. "Have you been to New York?" I ask, needing to move the subject away from my lies about The Backstreet Boys.

"No, but I always thought that maybe I would end up there some day."

"It's a great city. I never thought I'd end up living in Los Angeles but I've been out here for almost nine years now."

Her phone beeps. She ignores it, which makes me happy. I assume it is one of the other couples working with Jonathan.

Silence descends. First dates are exhausting.

"Have you seen any good movies?" I ask.

"I love movies, but I don't go out a lot. I like to rent movies."

Homebody, I scribble down.

"What have you rented lately?" I want to keep the conversation going and the other potential parents away.

"Austin Powers," she says, "I think Mike Myers is really funny. And I loved The Birdcage."

Beep.

"Me too," I say and white-knuckle the handset. I hated that movie with its prancing stereotypes. I do wonder if this is her way of letting me know she likes gay people.

Daniel drops his legal pad in front of me:

IF YOU COME HERE YOU WILL BE SAFE.

I shake my head and wave him back outside.

Her phone beeps again.

"Can I put you on hold? Someone keeps calling," Emma says.

"Of course," I say and immediately gulp down half a glass of water. I drink it too quickly and begin to choke.

"Are you all right?" Daniel appears at my side.

I nod. "I'm on hold," I sputter.

"You're doing really well," he says.

"What if the other call is from one of the other families?" I ask. I feel a connection with Emma and I don't like the idea of any of Jonathan's other clients calling her.

At our initial consultation, Jonathan went over the entire adoption process, step by step. In most cases, he told us, the birthmother contacts him; after he establishes her commitment level he determines what kind of a home she wants for her child: straight couple, same-sex couple, single parent, or interracial? I wondered how many birthmothers would consider a same-sex couple. He offers each birthmother three potential adoptive situations. The prospective families call her to plead their case. Then they wait.

This felt right to me—that the birthmother should be a proactive participant, making her own informed, conscious decision.

Jonathan also emphasized the importance of smiling during the conversation; he believes that warmth comes through the phone. He stressed that no matter what she says, we must express our unconditional support.

I send Daniel back outside.

While I wait for Emma to return, a shift occurs; I understand what I have to do. I must assure her we are prepared to be what she wants us to be. That we are prepared to be parents.

"Sorry about that," she says.

Will she tell me it was another potential adoptive family?

"It was my father."

Not another family. *Her* family. Her *father*.

What must that have been like for her, with me on the other line?

"No worries. Are you close with your parents?" I ask. "I'm quite close with mine. We spend every Christmas together."

Give information to get information.

"I'm really close to mine too," she says. "We get together every Sunday for dinner. That's one of the reasons I need to leave town. My parents don't know I'm pregnant and I am starting to show."

Scribbled: *parents don't know*

How close can they be?

She tells me she didn't know that it was an option to place her child with a same-sex couple until Jonathan brought it up, but she is very open to it. Her best friend is gay and *Will & Grace* is one of her favorite shows. I wonder if she wants me to be Sean Hayes, gayer and wittier. I wish I had a roomful of writers to help me out.

"We are so grateful that you are considering us," I tell her.

Silence.

Dammit. A writer would've come up with a better line.

"Daniel and I have been together for over six years," I say in an attempt to get information about the biological father. She has not mentioned him yet.

"That's a long time," she says.

Be direct.

"How did you meet the birthfather? What's his name?"

"Liam. We met in high school," she says, and I think I detect some distaste for him. "He was a year ahead of me. But we only dated last fall for a short time."

Liam, I write down. *Dated briefly – met in H.S.*

"How does he feel about the adoption?" I ask, trying to sound nonchalant.

"He told me he thought I should keep the baby."

The shortness in her tone confirms my gut feeling. She doesn't like him.

"But the last thing he told me was that 'adoption was the best thing.'"

Liam: Adoption best thing.

"Of course that was after he told me 'I was a walking piece of meat with no soul.'"

"How dare he! You're amazing." My tone is defensive. I don't hear Daniel until I see him charging into the kitchen, shaking his head. He scratches furiously on his legal pad.

I am indignant and press on.

"Any woman who makes a conscious decision, an adult decision, a decision that is best for someone else—your child—is extraordinary." I take a breath. "What you're doing is extraordinary."

Daniel throws his pad onto the island:

SMILE!!

UNCONDITIONAL LOVE!!!

If he only knew, I think.

I take a breath and force myself to smile.

"I think you are amazing," I say. "And I'm sorry he said that to you."

I hope she hears the honesty in my voice and not the forced smile on my face.

"We will take good care of you."

I look down and see Daniel's note from earlier. Now is the time.

"You'll be safe here."

She doesn't respond but I know it was the right thing to say.

"We made a book for you with some photos. It'll show you who we are, our families, things like that. We'd love to send it to you overnight."

"Sounds good," she says.

I tell her to call us any time and give her the 800-number Jonathan had us install. We say goodbye.

I am a sweaty, exhausted, exhilarated mess and Daniel hugs me.

"You did really well," he says and then pulls away, "but you smell like a truck driver."

FROM THE DEPOSITION OF LIAM FLYNN
JANUARY 2002

Q: What do you recall of your conversation with Emma on June 17th?

A: I remember telling her I wasn't—I was going to do everything in my power to have a chance of raising my child.

Q: At any point during Emma Murphy's pregnancy, do you remember telling her, if you think that's the best thing, she could go ahead and place the baby for adoption?

A: Yes.

Q: When was that?

A: Approximately three weeks later.

Q: Between the time you spoke with her on June 17th and the three weeks later conversation, what contact, if any, did you have with her?

A: I called her quite a bit. I was trying to get, you know, custody of my child and trying to work something out so that she wouldn't do that, give it away for adoption.

Q: Did you give her any money during this three-week period?

A: No.

Q: Did you offer any money?

A: I offered to pay for a trip to a doctor.

Q: Did you ever go to the doctor with her?

A: No, she refused.

Q: During the entirety of her pregnancy, did you give her any money?

A: No.

Q: Did you offer her any money other than what you already testified?

A: No.

Q: Did you ever buy her any maternity clothes?

A: No.

Q: What do you remember of what you said to her during the conversations when you were trying to convince her not to place the baby for adoption?

A: I tried saying maybe we could work something out. Maybe we could still like see each other again, or I tried everything. I tried if I could get custody, if she would sign over rights.

Q: Did you ever make any arrangements—did you suggest any arrangements for her during that three-week period whereby she could keep the baby and you would pay child support?

A: No. I tried everything.

Q: Excuse me?

A: I never made any arrangements, no.

8

"I'd like you to call Nicole Morgan," Jonathan tells us the following morning. September has never moved slower. Each day feels like two. "She is the best adoption litigator in California." There is a brief pause and then he adds, "Best to make some arrangements. Just in case."

I fight off the urge to climb back into bed and pull the covers over my head. When I was eight, I hid underneath my parent's blanket when the flying monkeys appeared in *The Wizard of Oz*. But even as a child I knew that the scary part would come to an end. Now I have no idea.

Daniel, on the other hand, is having a take no prisoner's day.

He dials Nicole's number. I make up an excuse to care for Zelda.

"I need to make a bottle before she wakes up," I tell him. I know the narrative we need to lay out for Nicole, and I don't want to hear it again.

"All we know is what he said to Jonathan," I hear Daniel say after he introduces himself to Nicole.

I check in on Zelda. We missed the lesson about how much

babies sleep during the first few weeks. It is remarkable. How blessed she is to be oblivious to all that has happened in the world these last couple of days.

"Yes," I hear Daniel say, "Liam told Jonathan he is planning on contesting the adoption."

In the kitchen I stop and listen, unable to walk away. I have a child now. This is all a part of the new "we." I can't hide under covers anymore.

"The last thing he told Emma was that adoption was the best option," Daniel says, which is followed by a lot of listening.

I wonder if Daniel is telling her everything, if he is spinning the tale to our best advantage. But I chose not to be on the call. And really Daniel is brilliant with spin; he is a storyteller by trade. Half-listening may make me insane so I go outside, away from Daniel's voice, from the call, from our new reality. He will fill me in on everything soon enough.

Our fig tree has just started to produce fruit and I sit myself down on the small iron bench under its branches. It is good to be outside, away from the daily necessities and demands. Away from the endless analyses of our situation. I recall Emma's words: *You are her parents*. I will remind myself of these words at two o'clock in morning when I warm Zelda's formula. *You are her parents*, I will mumble as I change Zelda's diaper and kiss her soft belly. *You are her parents*, I will think when I bundle her into her Bjorn and walk her through our neighborhood, one hand on her tiny back. *You are her parents*, I will tell myself when I bring her to her next pediatric appointment.

We are her parents.

The sun rejuvenates me. Stepping away allows me to catch my breath. I hear Daniel's muffled voice and wonder how long he has been on the phone, how much time has passed. I lost track. Time has taken on a life of its own since Zelda arrived. Time is a shape shifter. Was it really only six months ago that Daniel and I first seriously talked about wanting children?

∼

"I think I would actually enjoy being pregnant," I tell Daniel as I pull up my sleep shirt and extend my stomach, "too bad I'm not a sea horse."

It is March 2001 and just after eight in the morning, but still dark outside and surprisingly cold. Neither of us wants to get out of bed. It is a workday so I am surprised that Daniel is still in bed and not yet writiing; he is religious about his schedule. Sadie lies sprawled on the end of our bed and keeps our feet warm; perhaps she is trying to keep us here.

"Hi," I say as he turns to face me.

"Hey."

The stillness is lovely.

"I think I'm ready to have a child," I say. "I know we've talked around it, but—"

"Me too." he says, not missing a beat. "I want to be a young parent. But Ben?" His use of my name in conversation makes me roll my eyes.

"*Daniel*," I say, pointing it out.

He knows I hate when people use my proper name. It feels condescending, makes me shut down.

"Babe," he continues, softening his tone, "I just want to make sure that you're ready. You know I work every day, so a lot of the child care will fall on your shoulders."

"I know."

"Are you ready for that?"

"I think I am."

Daniel furrows his brow.

"I am," I say. "Honestly, I am. I have been for a long time. As a matter of fact, I'm going to look into adoption options today. I'm gonna find us our baby."

I jump out of bed and run through the house singing, "I'm gonna find us a baby." Sadie leaps off our bed and chases after me.

I situate myself at the dining table with my computer, a pad and a pen. A cup of warm tea feels good in my hands and I dig into a homemade blueberry muffin. Daniel and I are pretty certain that we are going to pursue an open adoption, where the birth parents and the adoptive parents are "open" to ongoing contact. We know firsthand that secrets lead to lies, which lead to shame, which leads to guilt, and we want no part of that.

A friend mentioned an organization called The Pop Luck Club. I find the play on words both irritating and intriguing. I open their website to read that it is the "largest known gay fathers' organiza-tion in the world." Its mission: "the advancement and well-being of gay prospective parents and their children...through mutual support, community collaboration, and public understanding."

I stare at the screen. My knee-jerk reaction is to shut the computer and never look back. Group mentality makes me want to run screaming for the hills. *Lord of the Flies* never seems far off. Still, the obvious pro-gay/father mandate is impossible to ignore. Many gay men would rightfully find themselves drawn to such an inclusive group but I have never been a joiner. There are many people, gay and straight, who find self-definition in their sexuality. I am not one of them. I do not self-identify first and foremost as a gay man. Perhaps that's a consequence of growing up in the 1970s. Perhaps it was my profound fear of contracting AIDS in the 1980s or perhaps it was having liberal parents who had a difficult time coming to terms with having a gay son. But for whatever reason, I am wary of this organization.

I sit and gaze at the screen and unconsciously devour my muffin.

"What's that?" Daniel asks. He appears out of nowhere and leans down to look at my screen.

"A group for gay men seeking children."

As soon as the words come out of my mouth I realize it's ludicrous *not* to explore it further.

"Wow. And you love groups," he laughs. "Where are they?"

"In the Valley."

"Seriously?" Daniel asks.

The group meets not far from our house. It could not be more convenient.

He tells me to email them and walks out of the room.

Daniel does not waste time. He figures out what he needs, filters out any unnecessary noise and completes the task at hand. He is a gatherer, foraging for information, utilizing all that he needs and then moving on. I, on the other hand, tend to over-analyze every situation. I wonder who someone is, how they got to this or that point, why they think the way they do and what they want. He falls asleep as soon as his head hits the pillow; I stay awake for hours pondering his ability to do that.

I send them an email, go to a yoga class, buy food for dinner; by the time I get home there is a reply in my inbox. The Pop Luck Club meets the following weekend, and we are welcome to attend.

On a clear and sunny day a week later, Daniel and I pull up in front of a small, Ranch-style house in the San Fernando Valley. He is absolutely at ease. I, on the other hand, am gripped by equal parts anxiety and desire. I want this so badly and I worry my expectations will never be met. I'm so convinced this will be a dead-end rather than a beginning that I try to cut my losses.

"I'll do more research," I stammer. "I'm sure I can find whatever information they might have here somewhere online."

"Ben."

"You're so young," I say. I sound ridiculous but I press on. "Too young. You're only thirty-one. That's too young to parent. And I'm too old." Everything that comes out of my mouth is fear-based.

How can you be a father?

Do one's demons ever really go away?

Daniel ignores me and parks the car.

"We're going in," he says.

Someone has scotch-taped a handwritten sign to the front door of the house. It's lettered in crayon by a child: "Come on in!"

Too earnest, I think. Too adorable. Too perfect.

"Come on..." Daniel laughs. He knows how badly I want this *and* how much I want to walk away.

The front door is unlocked and the house is quiet. There is no hint of life; were it not for the sign on the door I would have thought we were entering the wrong home.

We make our way through the dining room. There is a random selection of food on the table. Chips Ahoy cookies on a white paper plate, tortilla chips in a large glass bowl, and a half empty jar of salsa. I see crumbs on the table.

"Maybe we are in the wrong home," I joke. "What self-respecting gay man offers such a weak spread?"

Daniel laughs and pushes me inside.

We have come to find our child. This is the first step.

The sound of voices pulls Daniel and me toward the back of the house. We come to the end of a hallway and find ourselves in a living room with large glass doors flung open, revealing a yard full of people. The sight of thirty men, all of whom want to be fathers, stops me in my tracks.

Allow life to surprise you.

A few couples have children who scurry about, but most of the men are, like us, at the beginning of their journeys. The sight of all these men united by a desire to raise children has a visceral effect on me. It fills me with hope; it excites me and terrifies me.

My long-held dream of having a child stares me in the face.

"How are you doing?" I feel Daniel's hand on the curve of my back.

"I'm good." I repeat. "Cautiously optimistic."

We walk out into the yard and I notice most of the men are older by at least a decade. There are only two women. One is tall and blond and clearly pregnant. She looks as if she would be happier home in bed. The other woman has the vibe of someone whose best friend is always a gay man—there is nowhere she would rather be.

The couple and their surrogate approach us. After they introduce themselves, the woman kindly excuses herself. "I have to pee all the time now," she says and goes inside. Daniel and I discussed surrogacy but neither of us felt the need to be a part of the genetic creation of our child. And unlike a straight couple, a gay couple must ultimately choose one or the other to be the biological parent.

The two men look so similar: short hair, too much gym-time, spray tans; I have already forgotten their names.

Tan Man One leans in and whispers, "We really wanted to use our own sperm, choose the egg donor, really *know* where the baby was coming from."

His conspiratorial tone confuses me. And why was he whispering?

"We want to be able to understand our child," Tan Man Two says, without a hint of irony.

"People will tell you otherwise," Tan Man One says, leaning in, "but trust us, surrogacy is the way to go."

I want to be far away from these men.

"We're adopting," I tell them.

"Oh." Tan Man One says. His eyes blink rapidly, as though he is unable to comprehend what I am saying.

"Well...good luck with that," says Tan Man Two, a tight smile spread across his face.

Daniel and I hustle away.

"What was *that?*" I ask Daniel.

"I have no idea," he laughs, "but they freak me out."

We meet a single Asian man in the middle of a foster-to-adopt program. Daniel and I had contemplated going down this road but decided we wanted a baby.

"I always knew I wanted to foster-adopt. There are so many children stuck in the system and I can give them things they've never dreamed of, you know?"

He looks at us with such vulnerability that everything becomes clear. All of us want the same thing. We want to be fathers and our options are few and far between. It is 2001 and gay parenting is new. We are each seeking validation, affirmation, some sign that the choices we are making are the right ones. These men are pioneers, forging the way for those who will follow. And I am one of them.

"We have friends who went through the foster care system and loved it," Daniel says kindly.

"Good luck," I say.

"Hello, everyone. Hello?" The group quiets.

"I'm Michael and this is Luca." Michael is in his early fifties and smiles down at his son, who must be around three years old. Luca hides his face behind his father's leg. "I want to welcome you all to another Pop Luck Club."

An awkward smattering of applause.

Michael reaches down and lifts his son onto his hip where the boy rests his head on his father's shoulder. This makes me smile.

"I'm going to ask that we all make a large circle," Michael says, "so that we can go around and find out why we're all here and what we're looking for."

"A fucking circle?" I whisper to Daniel.

"We just need to find a lawyer," he responds.

"I'm Steve," says the man to the left of Michael. "My partner Bill and I are *just* starting to think about all of this. Until recently, it seemed impossible. Anyway, we would love to talk to anyone who will share their story with us."

"Hi, my name is Stan. I'm single...and looking."

People laugh.

"Seriously though," Stan continues, "I think I am ready to have a child. I would love to talk to any single people here who have done it or are thinking of doing it or...are looking for a date."

People laugh again.

Daniel ignores it all. When I began researching adoption, Jonathan Ross's name kept popping up. Our hope was to find someone with firsthand knowledge of him. We also wanted to get the name of at least one more lawyer.

The circle continues. It's almost our turn; my palms begin to sweat. I dislike speaking in front of groups.

"I'm Daniel and this is Ben," I hear Daniel say. He speaks for both of us. I want to throw my arms around him and thank him for knowing me so well. "We're looking for anyone who might have worked with a lawyer named Jonathan Ross. But we would like to know about other lawyers in L.A. who specialize in open adoptions as well. Thanks."

Then the man to my right introduces himself.

Leaning into Daniel, I whisper, "You are going to be a great father."

Two couples approach us after everyone has spoken.

One couple speaks highly of Jonathan; they are waiting to connect with a birthmother.

"How long have you been waiting?" I ask.

"About six months," one of them says.

"Actually seven," the other corrects. "But that's normal," he says reassuringly, as much for his partner's benefit as for ours. "Jonathan is the best though."

We get the name of a lawyer in Marina Del Ray from another couple. I am fascinated that both lawyers are men.

Armed with this information, Daniel and I make our way back through the house, past the now crusty salsa jar and the paper plates littered with cookie crumbs. When I shut the door behind me I notice the "Come on in" sign has fallen onto the "Welcome" doormat. I bend down and pick it up, press the scotch tape into the door and rehang the sign.

∼

A shadow falls across my eyes and for a moment I can't remember where I am. I can't recall what's happening and why I am outside in our yard.

Baby brain, I think.

I open my eyes. Daniel stands above me. Everything floods back; the pit in my stomach returns.

"Nicole says we need to sit tight and see if he really does anything."

"Not incredibly helpful," I mumble. "Did you like her?"

"I guess. Hard to tell over the phone. She's sending us a bunch of California Supreme Court cases to read. She says the cases will be helpful for us. She also said we need to keep Emma in Los Angeles as long as possible."

"She's not going to like that."

"I told her that. But she said her biggest concern right now is Liam filing a paternity and custody action in Minnesota."

"I don't understand anything you are saying," I tell him.

"Neither did I." He laughs softly. "She said if he does file anything in Minnesota we would be faced with having to establish California jurisdiction. The problem is they are both from Minnesota *and* Zelda was conceived there."

"It only gets better," I say.

"She was pretty adamant that we want to fight this in California and *not there*. So keeping Emma here as long as possible is best." He pauses. "I heard Zelda waking up. I'll get her."

I can't help but feel that the world has gone mad. It all seems insane—Daniel and I becoming parents, Liam threatening to contest the adoption, 9/11—where was *this* chapter in *What to Expect When You Are Expecting?*

From the yard I can hear Daniel's voice and I wonder if he is back on the phone with Nicole. But then I see him walk into the kitchen with Zelda in his arms. They are briefly at the sink and then gone from view. But his voice drifts outside:

"Should we read a story? Should we read *King & King?*"

I picture him sitting on the rocking chair with Zelda in his lap. In one hand he holds the book; with the other he feeds her.

I remember my father reading to me from a large Grimm Fairytale book. Now I think of Liam as Rumplestiltskin, the devil come to snatch my child.

FROM THE DEPOSITION OF LIAM FLYNN
JANUARY 2002

Q: Do you remember having some telephonic contact with attorney Jonathan Ross?

A: Correct. He asked me what my—if I had gotten the paperwork he had sent.

Q: Do you remember telling him that you were not going to oppose the adoption, but you weren't going to sign anything?

A: I told him I wasn't sure what I was going to do—there was a possibility that I would do nothing.

Q: You had Mr. Ross's telephone number, correct?

A: Yes.

Q: Between July 13th and September 8th, did you ever call Mr. Ross back?

A: Yeah.

Q: Before the baby was born?

A: No. No. After the baby was born.

Q: Is it fair to say that before the baby was born, you didn't know what you were going to do in terms of opposing the adoption?

A: Yes.

Q: Between the time that Emma left for California and the time that the baby was born, what efforts, if any, did you make to try to get in touch with Emma?

A: None.

Q: Did you ever tell Emma in any way between the time that you told her that maybe adoption was the best thing and the time that you filed your paternity action that you were going to oppose the adoption?

A: No, I didn't.

Q: You spoke with Emma ten days after the baby was born. Did you ask her any questions about where the baby was during that conversation?

A: No.

Q: Did you ask her where she was?

A: No.

Q: Have you made any arrangements to reimburse either Emma or the adoptive parents for any of her maternity-related expenses?

A: No.

Q: When you and Emma were having a sexual relationship, what kind of birth control, if any, was being used?

A: Condoms occasionally.

Q: And occasionally not?

A: Occasionally not, correct.

Q: Calling your attention to the September 12th conversation with Jonathan Ross, your sister had emailed Mr. Ross, isn't that correct?

A: Yes.

Q: That was before you contacted Mr. Ross, correct?

A: Yes.

Q: Why was your sister contacting Mr. Ross, if you know?

A: That's the kind of person she is.

Q: What do you mean?

A: She likes to get her nose in things.

9

I wake up alone. Our anniversary, September 18th, is five days away. I know we should mark it, but the idea of celebrating is difficult right now. Daniel must have snuck out with Zelda when she woke up. I am surprised that I slept through it. It is just after nine in the morning.

In the bathroom, I glance out of the window into the yard. Daniel has Zelda in his arms. He is too far back for me to hear him but I see his mouth moving and the smile on his face. I am filled with joy, a joy immediately tempered by my ever-present anxiety. These two sensations may co-exist for some time.

"Good morning," I say, as I join them outside.

Zelda turns her head toward me and I reach out and take her in my arms. Is it possible at this age that she recognizes my voice? I decide she does.

"Hi angel," I say and kiss her face.

"What about me?" Daniel asks.

"Hi," I add, and kiss him too. "Thanks for letting me sleep."

"I called Emma. I wanted to make sure she remembered I was coming at ten," Daniel says as he heads back into the house.

Legally, Emma has thirty days to terminate her parental rights, but California offers every birthmother the option to waive her rights after three days. Emma always maintained that she would sign the waiver, but because of 9/11, the third day actually falls on the fifth day of Zelda's life. Her appointment is at eleven this morning. We had planned to celebrate, open champagne, raise a glass to Emma, and express our gratitude for everything. Now that celebration will have to wait.

Or perhaps never happen.

Emma's paperwork is now just one piece of a puzzle that is far from complete. It does give us something to hold onto though, and for that I am grateful.

Oddly enough, Liam also has thirty days. He must legally contest the adoption within that time period or he forfeits his rights.

He is down to twenty-five days.

"Did you talk to Emma about staying longer?" I ask Daniel as we enter the kitchen.

"She said she'll stay a little bit more, but not a lot," he adds and starts in on his morning snack of Greek yogurt and fruit. "She wants to go home."

She wants to get back to her life, and we feel conflicted about pressing her to stay. She has kept her word. She has done what she promised to do. But her definitive declaration unsettles me. I have come to depend upon her presence. Her conviction about placing Zelda for adoption has never wavered and I have drawn strength from that. Now, I realize, that must be enough. I have to let her go. Whatever comes is no longer her job or her responsibility. We have no right to ask her to stay.

"How much longer do they want her here?" I ask.

"No one will say."

I hear an edge in his voice. We know nothing, have no answers, nor any control - and it makes us edgy.

"I know I slept in," I say and follow him into the dining room, "but would you watch her for five more minutes? I can't remember the last time I washed my hair."

What I really need is time alone.

"I would love to," Daniel says, addressing Zelda directly. "What should we do?" he asks as he takes her from my arms.

The warm water helps but Emma's coming departure combined with Liam's lingering threat and the aftermath of 9/11 has unsettled me. I can't shake the pressure behind my eyes, like a dam holding back water for too long. Am I experiencing post-partum without giving birth? I had one life with Daniel; now we are three and the world is so different. Fragile. The city I grew up in was attacked. A sense of security taken for granted, forever gone. How does one—how do I—raise a child in this post-terrorist world? How do I keep her safe? The tears mix with the shower water. The release feels good.

As I emerge from the bathroom, I see Daniel hanging up the phone. All the tension immediately returns.

"Jonathan just called to check in," Daniel says, seeing my obvious anxiety. "He mentioned some letter he sent to Liam back in July..." and trails off as he hands me the letter he must have dug out while I was in the shower.

> Notice of Alleged Paternity – July 6, 2001
> To: Liam Flynn, alleged father:
> PLEASE TAKE NOTICE that it is alleged that you are, or could be, the natural father of the above-mentioned child, due to be born on or about September 7, 2001 to Emma Murphy.
> PLEASE TAKE FURTHER NOTICE that, pursuant to California Family Code sections 7631 and 7662, your failure to bring an action within 30 days after the birth of said child or service of this notice upon you, whichever last occurs, for the purpose of declaring that you are the father of the above mentioned child may result in the child's being legally adopted by others without further notice to you.

"He never responded to it," Daniel says, his voice strained.

"Weird how this meant nothing at the time. It all felt so abstract."

"Not abstract anymore," Daniel adds.

We all took Liam's silence as his answer. Now, with one phone call, he has thrust us into litigation and absolute uncertainty. We will raise Zelda with no guarantee that she will remain ours.

"Let me get dressed," I tell him, "then I'll take Zelda."

Things are coming at us so fast it is difficult to keep everything in order. I continue to hope that Liam will come to his senses or that his sister will ease off and this will all just disappear. His last-minute change of mind simply makes no sense. I pull on my t-shirt and wonder whether either of my sisters would have stepped in if I had fathered a child (odds are against it, as I only slept with two women). But it begs the question: does the ability to create a life give you ownership over that life?

Daniel walks into our room and sees me sitting on our bed, a corner of Jonathan's letter crushed in my hand.

"What happened to you?" he asks.

"Sorry," I say and take Zelda in my arms. "I am glad we went with Jonathan," I add.

Daniel eyes the letter in my hand and pauses. "I'll be in the back. I have to send my script in."

We wrestle with when to engage with one another's anxiety and fear and when to leave it alone.

I sit on our bed with Zelda in my arms and think about the decisions that led us to her, each choice affirming what we know in our hearts: she was meant to be our child.

And she *is* ours.

What role does fate play in this?

Had we not hired Jonathan would we have found Zelda? Would we have met Emma some other way?

Zelda squirms.

"Let's get you a bottle," I say and head into the kitchen.

I think back on our first meeting with Jonathan and how little we knew, how naïve we were.

~

Never ones to waste time, a week after the Pop Luck Club meeting Daniel and I are in the underground parking lot of the Century City Mall. We are early for our eleven o'clock appointment with Jonathan Ross. His assistant seemed taken aback by our request to meet him—evidently few vet him, his reputation is that good. But we are that thorough.

"I'm nervous," I mutter.

"I know. Me too," Daniel says.

Neither of us make a move. Once we step out of the car it is only a matter of time before we have a child.

"It's like we're about to pee on that little plus-minus stick thing and see if we're pregnant."

"Hey now," Daniel jokes and opens his door, "we don't even

know if we want to be in bed with this guy."

"Fair enough," I say and follow him out of the parking structure into the sprawling mall. In order to get to the office building where Jonathan works, we must walk through the Ann Taylor store. As we purposefully stride through the racks of conservative clothes, I imagine all the previous prospective parents who made their way through this store. I wonder if the bored workers can pick them out—pick us out—all these non-customers, these apprehensive, potential parents passing through, not browsing, not asking for help. I wonder if they can detect our anxiety and our hope.

The elevator speeds up to the 19th floor and my ears pop.

"This is one of those remember-when moments."

"Another beginning," Daniel says.

"How crazy is all of this?" I ask as the doors open.

A receptionist greets us with a smile that seems to read, "Oh, so *you're* the Type A vetters," before she nods us toward the marble waiting area. We sit and reach for the thumbed-through magazines that lie on the coffee table. After a few minutes, the double glass doors open and Jonathan Ross appears. He is tall and has a lumbering gate; I am reminded of Robert DeNiro.

"Nice to meet you, gentlemen," he says, and extends his hand.

Jonathan's office is spacious and warm and has floor-to-ceiling windows looking out over Beverly Hills. He sits behind an oversized wooden desk and we sit in two chairs. Photographs of children line the bookshelves and countertops. I spy a box of children's toys tucked away in a corner.

"So what can I do for you guys?" Jonathan asks.

"Well, we want to adopt..." Daniel tells him with a brief, uncomfortable laugh. "I mean, obviously."

"An open adoption," I add. "We want to know how it all works."

"Well it's pretty straightforward," Jonathan says briskly. "A birthmother finds me, either through a reference or yellow pages. Once I establish what kind of a family she's looking for, I contact you and try to make a match."

"Do you start with one family at a time?" I ask.

"No. I normally give her three options. I like her to have a choice."

"How long does the process take?"

"Typically it's between six months and a year and a half."

"How long have you been doing adoptions?" Daniel asks.

"Twenty-five years."

"And what made you get into this kind of law?"

"I like to win," he responds without missing a beat.

He likes to win? I think.

We are talking about babies here, about birthmothers, about our potential child. I stop listening to what he says next and fixate on his response—it feels crass, like it somehow cheapens the process.

"Well, thank you for taking the time to sit down with us," I hear Daniel say after several minutes.

Twenty minutes after meeting Jonathan we are back in the elevator.

"What the fuck does that mean, I like to win?"

"I have no idea," Daniel says as we head back through Ann Taylor and down the escalator to our car, "but he seems like a straight shooter."

"Well...yeah...but...I like to *win*?" I mumble.

"Really though, don't we want to win?" Daniel counters as we head out of the parking structure. "Don't we want a kid? And don't we want someone in our corner who will make that happen?"

Somewhere along my way, I internalized the idea that to claim this desire was wrong. Perhaps it happened that one Thanksgiving night so many years ago, when my demons reared their ugly heads. Perhaps it was growing up without a single role model: I believed I could never be a father *and* a gay man; I was certain of it.

I am angry to discover that twenty years later, as an adult, these inner demons continue to live inside me. It is time to exorcise them once and for all. Beginning today I will ask for—rather, demand—what I want for myself.

I want a child.

I want to win.

~

Sadie barks; Zelda startles. The dog needs to go for a walk so I search for Zelda's Bjorn. It'll be good to get out, get fresh air; get out of my head.

"I'm going to pick up Emma," Daniel says, walking into the living room as I strap Zelda onto my chest. "I'll believe it when I see it, but she is about an hour away from signing her waiver."

I follow Daniel outside and walk into Hancock Park. Already I must strain to remember a time when Zelda was not a part of our lives. Her existence has altered everything.

Sadie stops abruptly and begins to bark. I look up and discover a woman across the street walking a miniature horse. Could this be a dream? Have I fallen down the rabbit hole? Black is white, left is right; perhaps this is the universe telling me I need to give into the absurdity, the unknown.

Excited to share the sighting with Zelda, I look down to discover that she has fallen asleep.

I marvel at babies' innate ability to take care of themselves. If Zelda needs sleep, she sleeps; if she is hungry, she cries.

I make a mental note to begin a list:

1. Put your own oxygen mask on first.

We leave the miniature horse and head home. My left hand remains pressed against her sleeping body. I love the nonverbal connection I have with her. I appreciate silence more than ever.

10

September 30th. Zelda is three weeks old.

Twenty-three. Twenty-two. Twenty-one.

The days pass without a word from Liam. We don't talk about it. We don't want to jinx anything.

Sixteen. Fifteen. Fourteen.

My eyes pop open. 1:54 AM. My internal clock now wakes me up just before Zelda, giving me the time I need to prep her bottle. She is gaining weight and growing more alert every day.

I take a moment before getting out of bed to watch her sleep. I imagine the walk we will take together later this morning. We walk every morning now and in the afternoons we nap. I lay her on my chest and allow the rhythm of my breath to lull us to sleep. I love to feel the weight of her small body as it rises and falls with each inhale and exhale. Sometimes I hold my breath so I can feel her belly press itself into mine. This is how I calm myself.

We have decided not to hire a nanny yet, so it is Zelda and me all day, every day. I am exhausted but happy.

I push myself out of bed and make my way into the kitchen. Before we went to sleep we filled the bottle with water; the precise amount of pre-measured formula sits next to it, just visible as moonlight fills the kitchen. After I warm the bottle in the microwave and shake it to get rid of any hot spots, I reenter our room, lift Zelda out of her Co-Sleeper, and carry her into the den. She latches onto the bottle as soon as I sit down on the glider. Everything is quiet. Everything is right. I drop into the stillness. Zelda fits so perfectly that I wonder if we were designed for each other.

The clock in the kitchen interrupts the solitude and ticks away: thir-teen, thir-teen, thir-teen. Liam has thirteen days left to file. If he doesn't, all of this goes away.

"Go away," I say into the darkness.

Zelda finishes the bottle and I lift her warm body onto my shoulder to burp her. How quickly the need to shield her from discomfort takes hold.

Her tiny head tucks into the crook of my neck. I record the sensation of her breath as it tickles my neck. I love that my outstretched hand can cover her entire back and I marvel at the power and efficiency of her tiny lungs. I drop my head and kiss the base of her soft neck. I ought to put her back to sleep but I don't want to let go.

What if I lose you?

I startle, as if the words had come from somewhere else.

What Liam has unleashed lurks, always there, like a clock you forget about and then suddenly hear.

"I have to get you back to bed," I say, making my way back down the hall to our bedroom, to Daniel and to sleep.

"Go away," I whisper, then fall asleep.

Thirteen.

Twelve.

My first thought when I wake up two days later: eleven more days.

As much as I want him out of my head, I can't help thinking about Liam, picturing him in Minnesota. I wonder what his house looks like, his room. In my mind, it is all grimy. His house is filthy, he is dirty: clothes are left on the floor, socks are bunched together under the bed, old and smelly. In my anger, I allow my classist prejudices to run wild. He lazes away his days in his tiny one-lane town. He watches nothing but sports and always needs the television on because he is antisocial. He hangs out at the local bar with the three guys he has known his whole life, all of whom secretly hate him. He ignores his sister nudging him to call the lawyer, preferring instead to hang out and shoot pool.

Tomorrow I will see Emma, take her to lunch. It can't be fun for her in Los Angeles, watching football and longing to be home. Does she think about time differently? Is there a post-birth shift in the way time moves for her as well? Does she marvel, like I do, that it was only three months earlier we spoke for the first time.

∽

I am a sweaty mess. I have just hung up with Emma after our first conversation. The call went well. Our cheat sheet lies before me scribbled with notes.

"You *do* realize you told her we would ship our book out tonight and FedEx closes in three hours?" Daniel asks. He does not attempt to hide the panic in his voice. "And the book doesn't actually exist yet."

The book does exist but in pieces scattered all over the house. We chose photos but never made copies of them; this is before the digital era, and we have to keep the originals in case it doesn't work out with Emma—or if we want to adopt again. We've written text to accompany the photos but we haven't printed any of it. We even chose a light blue baby fabric to cover the book, which we threw into the back of our closet for "safekeeping." And now we have three hours to put together the entire thing.

"Holy shit," I say, and we burst out laughing.

The prospect is daunting, the book being the least of it. Daniel was asleep an hour ago. Suddenly we might be seven and a half months pregnant.

"We can do this," I rally. We know two other families are talking to Emma, perhaps right now; surely their books are complete. More importantly, I promised Emma we would overnight her our book and I am determined to make good on my first promise to her.

Daniel jumps on the phone and finds a place that can print copies of our fifteen photos within the hour for twenty-dollars per photo, a total of three hundred dollars not including tax.

"Print the blurbs," he shouts as he heads out the door, "but on nice paper." He pops back in: "Oh and glue the fabric onto the book—and shit, do we still have the ribbon?"

It is four o'clock.

I tear his office apart before I locate a medium weight, pale ivory paper; while our text prints, I run back into the house and dig through our closet. I find the soft, fuzzy blue fabric with images of baby toys. Neither one of us would have ever chosen this fabric for ourselves but hope that it will speak to our birthmother. We bought a ribbon to tie around the book that reads: "*Home is where the Heart is.*" We may be hitting it too hard but then again, now is not the time for subtlety. Plus, with less than two hours, there is no time for second-guessing.

I race back across the yard to Daniel's office, Sadie nipping at my heels, aware something is happening. I grab the printed blurbs and head back into the house. Rereading the blurbs I am reminded of our second meeting with Jonathan. He made sure we understood that the biological mother may not have graduated high school and to keep it simple.

"We certainly did that," I hear myself mutter. Probably too sappy, I think, but Jonathan was insistent.

Back in the living room, I spread everything on the floor: blurbs, fabric, scissors, glue. I begin to cut and paste our story.

> Your Child Will Have Two Loving Daddies (accompanied by a smiling photo of Daniel and myself, in which we are touching which, according to Jonathan, was important; he also told us that the phrasing "Your Child" reassures the birthmother that she will always be the only "mother.")
>
> Ben is 36 years old. Raised in New York City, he is the youngest of three children. He graduated from a small college in Massachusetts. He designs handbags. His best seller is a diaper bag! Ben enjoys quilting, long walks with the dog and yoga. He is a wonderful baker and loves to have friends over for dinner and Sunday brunch. (*Could I sound more gay?*)
>
> Daniel is 32 years old. Raised in Philadelphia, he is the youngest of four children. He graduated from Yale University and then went to the University of Southern California's film school. He writes movies for children (*Partially true...he wrote one movie for children...though it was never made.*). Daniel likes swimming, gardening and reading.

He is great with the barbecue and friends call him the "grill master." (*Absolutely untrue.*)

Ben and Daniel volunteer to read to first, second and third graders every week. We live around the corner from a pretty library. Each week we choose new stories to read aloud. (Accompanied by a photo of each of us with our volunteer class; the subconscious message: *People trust us with their children and you should too!*)

Your child will be surrounded by lots of loving cousins. Together we have four nieces and two nephews. Once a month we have all our friends and their children over to our house for an all-day game playing and eating party. (Accompanied by a photo of Daniel with his nephews and nieces.)

We are blessed that we both work at home and make our own schedules! This means we can spend all the time we want with the baby. And best of all, our best friends live one block away with their adorable toddlers. In fact, we have a large group of friends who all live close by and help each other with their children. (Accompanied by a photo of me with my nieces and nephews.)

We have been together for over six years. Two years ago we had a commitment ceremony with both our families and all our friends. We are very excited to adopt a child. We know from our siblings and friends what it takes to raise children and we are ready! We think of adoption as a gift.

We have a beautiful home to offer your child. Our big yard has an apricot tree, a fig tree and a lemon tree. There is lots of room to run around and a big, friendly sheepdog named Sadie to roll around with! Our house has two bedrooms and also a playroom. There are lots of children on our quiet street playing hopscotch and tag.

Los Angeles is a great city for children. The beach is very close by and there are lots of parks. We love to go on hikes. Plus, there's Disneyland and Universal Studios! We also like to go on trips outside of California and are excited to show our child the world (*We almost never go to the beach. Disneyland is our worst nightmare.*)

We want a child more than anything in the world. We are ready to shower that child with love and affection. This book is only the tip of the iceberg. We can't wait to share more with you.

Daniel bursts through the front door at five o'clock with photos in hand.

"FedEx closes in one hour," he says as he drops the photos on the floor and races back to his office to write a letter to Emma to accompany the book. Jonathan told us the letter must be handwritten.

My eyes check the clock. We have twenty minutes to finish the book and get ourselves to FedEx.

At 5:40 we review the book page by page.

At 5:50 we tear out of the house.

At 5:58 we fly into FedEx. I grab a box while Daniel fills out a slip.

"Can I help you?" the woman behind the counter asks, obviously ready to go home.

"This will arrive tomorrow, right?" I ask as we hand over the box.

She manages a brief "uh-huh," slaps the receipt down, tosses the box into the bin behind her and shuts down her computer.

It is the first time either of us has stopped in three hours and we stand still for a brief moment.

For the first time, she looks at us. Her smile is gentle.

"You can track it online," she says, "and it *will* get there tomorrow."

The next day, I obsessively track the package.

Package arrived at station 9:03 AM. Package departed station 12:05 PM. Package scheduled for delivery 2:30 PM. Package left outside front door 3:52 PM.

I keep myself busy doing nothing and pretend I am not waiting for the phone to ring.

Night falls and we have heard nothing. I stand at the kitchen sink and rinse broccoli for dinner. I am worried by Emma's silence. I have good instincts. I know we had a real connection but—

"Ben!"

I glance outside and see Daniel running across the yard.

The phone is ringing. I drop the broccoli into the sink and use the kitchen doorframe to catapult myself down the short hallway into the TV room and grab the phone.

"Hello?" I shout. "Hello," I say again, trying to sound more relaxed.

"Hi, it's Emma."

"How are you doing?" I ask as Daniel flies into the room.

How do you think she is fucking doing? She is seven months pregnant, her family doesn't know and she is desperate to leave town.

"I got your book," she says. "I wanted to let you know that."

Silence.

"I'm glad you got it," I say.

"I really liked it," she says.

Here we go, I think, and my heart picks up speed. But only silence follows.

"Do you have any questions after having seen it?"

"No, not really."

"Well, we loved putting it together for you," I say.

"Okay. I just wanted you to know that. Bye." She hangs up. I am left flustered, the phone pressed against my ear.

"But what was her tone?" Daniel asks imploringly, after I reenact the brief conversation.

"I don't know. All she kept saying was that she liked it."

We walk back into the kitchen.

"She didn't have to call," I say. "Right?"

I retrieve the limp broccoli from the sink and notice that something has shifted inside of me. There is an expansiveness I don't recognize. A sense of possibility. I silently allow that truth to burrow itself into my heart.

The following day is Sunday. We stay home but she doesn't call.

Monday afternoon the phone rings.

"Hi, Emma."

There is a brief pause. Daniel looks at me.

She has to say it.

"I choose you. I want you to adopt the baby."

Images flash, fast and furious, in my mind's eye: me, on a stool wearing a crown, smiling up at the camera before blowing out nine candles, one for good luck. My sisters and I running on a boardwalk in Fire Island. Daniel slipping a ring on my finger beneath our chuppah.

I think I hear Daniel say my name and I come back to the room, back to the moment, back to Daniel.

"She'd like us to adopt her baby," I say and sit down on the couch. "I know this is a big decision," I tell her, "and I promise we will take good care of you and your baby."

Daniel has a massive grin plastered on his face.

"Thank you for making this dream come true for us," I add.

"Okay," she says quietly.

"I think you are extraordinary," I tell her.

She is silent and I feel self-conscious.

"I need to come as soon as possible," she says. Her tone is practical; she knows how to take care of herself. "I am beginning to show and need to leave town."

"Of course. We'll start making arrangements immediately and will call you back tomorrow."

How do I say goodbye to someone who gives you a child?

"Thank you, Emma."

Daniel joins me on the couch and takes my hand.

I believe your child finds you.

11

October, finally.

Nine. Eight. Seven.

Zelda has her one-month birthday. I take her to the pediatrician; he weighs and measures her and sticks a long needle into her small arm. I worry the point of the needle will come out the other side. The doctor declares that she is "thriving," and I wonder if we should put him on a list as a potential character witness.

Six.

The phone rings just as I put Zelda down for her nap. Daniel is in his office. I can see him sitting in his big writing chair with his computer on his lap.

"Liam filed a custody action today," Jonathan tells me. "He filed paperwork this morning with the Circuit Court Family Branch in Minnesota. I'm going to fax you a copy."

I force myself to remain calm, even as I feel my lips tighten and my eyes tear. Breathe.

"It looks like we this isn't going away. I'm sorry."

"Okay."

What else can I say?

His tone is sad and the news is upsetting but there is something liberating about hearing him finally just say it out loud. We have been in this waiting game for too long. That we finally know what is happening is almost a relief. This is not going away. We now have to deal with it.

We have no friends, gay or straight who have adopted. We are pioneers, I remind myself. We are breaking down barriers, forging new paths. It is isolating and lonely.

"Nicole wants you to call a man named Scott Foster today. He's a lawyer in Minnesota. She speaks highly of him. His sole job will be to get the jurisdiction moved to California. California's laws are very strong for adoptive parents so the need to get jurisdiction moved here is critical. Nicole said I couldn't emphasize this point enough. She also assures me that Scott is very good."

All I can do is listen. He gives me Scott's number. I write it down on the back of a receipt I find lying on the kitchen counter. It's from Target: *Diapers. Formula. Wipes. Two onesies. A bottle brush.*

Jonathan does not seem to expect any kind of response.

"I know this is hard," he says with genuine kindness in his voice, "but I do know that Zelda is your daughter. So stay strong."

"Thanks, Jonathan," I say, "for everything."

Daniel walks into the dining room with a copy of Liam's paperwork in his hand. Our fax machine is set up in his office. His hard expression reflects my own.

The Petitioner Requests the following relief:
A. The petitioner be adjudicated the father
   of the minor child.
B. The petitioner have sole legal custody and primary
   physical placement of the minor child.
C. Child Support
D. Such other relief as is appropriate

"What the fuck does he mean by child support?" Daniel asks. His tone is harsh. "By who? By us? By Emma? Is he fucking insane?"

We are screaming into the dark and totally depleted, and it is not even nine in the morning. We pass the brief note back and forth as we sit down on the couch in the living room and read it over and over again.

I wrestle with understanding what makes someone a parent.

Are you a parent because you create a life or are you a parent because you guide the life?

"Do you think it is possible," I ask Daniel, "just to close the curtains and hide? Maybe I can just stay indoors with Zelda forever and we can never answer the door."

Daniel lets out a slow, heartbreaking breath and we remain seated for what feels like an eternity, both of us uncertain how to proceed. We look like strangers in a waiting room.

"Now what?" I ask.

"Now we fight."

FROM THE DEPOSITION OF LIAM FLYNN
JANUARY 2002

Q: What do you recall of your conversation with Emma Murphy on June 17th?

A: I remember telling her I wasn't—I was going to do everything in my power to have a chance of raising my child.

Q: How long did that conversation last?

A: Roughly two hours.

Q: Between the time you spoke with her on June 17th and the three-weeks-later conversation, what contact, if any, did you have with her?

A: I called her quite a bit.

Q: Did you speak with her?

A: Yes.

Q: What do you remember of those conversations?

A: I was trying to get, you know, custody of my child and trying to work something out so that she wouldn't do that, give it away for adoption.

Q: What do you remember of what you said to her during the conversations when you were trying to convince her not to place the baby for adoption?

A: I tried saying maybe we could work something out. Maybe we could still like see each other again, or I tried everything. I tried to see if I could get custody, if she would sign over rights.

Q: Did you make any arrangements? Did you suggest any arrangement to her during that three-week time period whereby she could keep the baby and you would pay child support?

A: No. I tried everything.

Q: Excuse me?

A: I never really made any arrangements, no.

Q: Did you ever make any arrangements like that?

A: I made all kinds of suggestions.

Q: What did you suggest along those lines?

A: Along the lines of paying child support?

Q: Correct.

A: She didn't want to raise a child. There wasn't much to say. I tried. She didn't want it.

Q: Did you offer to raise the child?

A: I offered to raise the child myself, yes.

12

In the fall of 1989, Roxy Saturdays was in its heyday. It was hands down the hottest gay dance club in New York City. Located on 18th Street just blocks from the river, it was near the meatpacking district before the area became gentrified and Chelsea Market-ed. A small group of us would dance until the lights came up. The sight of beautiful shirtless men, all absolutely free, utterly unself-conscious about their sexuality, and all showing up to celebrate themselves and one another, shifted my self-perception. Each week I would feel more and more myself. I seldom left with anyone though there was the occasional tryst. Once, my youthful intelligence (when is it that the frontal cortex fully develops in men?) convinced me it was wise to spend the night with a man solely because he lived in the West Village where I had an early morning meeting the following day. At the time, it seemed like a smart bargain. But I was always looking for a relationship, so more often than not our small group would emerge into the pre-dawn glow of Chelsea and say our goodbyes or head off to the Florent diner for an early breakfast. I was twenty-three years old and my biggest concern was absolutely nothing. I had almost no obligations. I lived rent-free, I was single, I had a tight-knit group of friends, and I waited tables for extra money. Everything seemed possible; I had no one to answer to and few who expected anything from me.

That is no longer the case.

The following morning is cool for the middle of October. Daniel's words "now we fight" bounce around my head as I close the door to the backyard. The chill in the air reminds me of New York, and I find myself nostalgic for a life lived many years ago; perhaps I long for a time with fewer cares.

It is the first time in my life where I have taken on a responsibility that I cannot walk away from. This commitment is for life. And at times that terrifies me.

"Let's call Scott," Daniel says, walking past me into the den.

I check on Zelda. The sound machine will drown out our voices. I don't want her to hear this. I don't want her to hear any of it.

Despite my anxiety, we are both moving slowly this morning. It was a long night. Zelda had been up more than usual. Two days ago we were presumptuous enough to think that we had something down, that we had *mastered* her schedule, some element of our child. Last night forced us to admit that we understand almost nothing. Or rather, it forced us to realize that a human life is forever changing. Perhaps the lesson is to let go. Perhaps not always having the answer is the answer.

"It's ringing," Daniel says from the den. "Pick up."

"Nicole called me earlier this morning," Scott Foster tells us. "I'm sorry you are in this situation but please know that I will do everything in my power to have the jurisdiction moved to California."

"We appreciate that," I tell him.

"Your daughter, I'm sorry I don't have my notes in front of me..."

"Zelda."

"Yes, great name, by the way."

"Thank you."

"Zelda was born in Los Angeles, right? And the birthmother?" he asks.

"Emma," Daniel interjects.

"Yes. Emma. She has been there since the middle of July, is that right?"

"That's right," I say as I walk into the den. I flash back to the moment in this very same room when Emma called to say she had chosen us. "She really doesn't want her family to find out about the pregnancy," I add, grabbing a blanket from the couch before I head outside. I need space and fresh air. The house feels claustrophobic.

"Understood."

"Emma has been unwavering from the get-go," Daniel tells him.

"I'm sure. Listen, I know you're anxious and I imagine you have a bunch of questions, but I am going to be late for court if I don't get off the phone." I hear him push his chair back and shuffle some papers as someone attempts to get his attention. "My retainer fee is $5,000 and my hourly rate is $215 an hour. I just like to get that out of the way. I'll call you tomorrow morning after reviewing all the notes and if you want to proceed we'll go from there."

"Very good," I say. "Can I just ask you one question?"

"Tomorrow. I'm sorry. I am already late for court. Tomorrow."

And he hangs up.

The blanket does nothing to keep the cold out so I head back indoors. Daniel and I exchange faint smiles, his face etched with exhaustion.

"You realize with his fee and Nicole's we'll have laid out ten thousand dollars in two days," Daniel says and places the phone back in its cradle.

What response is Daniel looking for?

Ten thousand dollars. That is a lot of money. But Zelda is our daughter and we know we will hire Scott. There is no plan B.

Money has always been a complicated issue for me. Men remain the presumed providers; not providing leaves me feeling inadequate. Daniel earns almost all our money and it causes a constant need within me to justify any expense. I feel pressure in our home and in society at large. It is a unique dynamic within the gay world. A "who wears the pants in the family/who is the top" question. The lines are blurred and can cause confusion. Parenting is my job but no one pays me for that. It is an identity but not a *job*. I play the traditional female role but I am not a woman. I straddle different worlds—not a part of the mommies-who-lunch group, nor part of the basketball-game-for-dads club. I remain apart from each. But that might be my choice as much as theirs.

"It's nerve-wracking putting our trust in someone we'll never meet," I say.

"*Hopefully* never meet," Daniel clarifies immediately and knocks three times on the wooden side table, his superstitious tendencies intensifying ever since Liam filed his lawsuit.

The question I wanted to ask Scott haunts me all day and into the night. By two-thirty in the morning I can't take it anymore. After feeding Zelda and putting her back to bed, I open my computer and let the blue glare from its screen cast a faint glow over the room. Sending an email in the middle of the night is never a good idea. And yet.

Email to Scott Foster:

I wanted to ask you if you thought our case might become a referendum on our sexuality, or gay parenting itself. We look forward to speaking with you later.

His response waits for me when I wake up a few hours later:

Email from Scott Foster:

Not a concern. You would not be a factor here. The focus is only on whether or not the rights of the father should be terminated.

"Even Emma said Liam doesn't care that we're gay," Daniel says when I tell him about the e-mail later that morning. "Plus, what are you doing e-mailing him at two in the morning?"

The question hangs in the air between us. We are in the midst of giving Zelda a bath, neither one of us quite ready to go it alone. We stand at the sink staring down at this small being.

Daniel is right. I knew it at the time, but I will take anything at this point to make me feel better, safer, less afraid.

"I really don't think this is a gay thing." Daniel says as he lifts Zelda out of the water. I wrap her warm body in a towel and think about whether I agree with him. Daniel is four years younger than I am, a lifetime in the gay landscape. Daniel has a theory that in the last forty years there has been a generational shift for gay people every half-decade—a seismic change both in cultural perception and how gay people view themselves. The experience for gays five years older than me is radically different from my own experience, which is radically different from the experience of those five years younger.

"It's tapping into all my old shit," I mutter and resent that my exhaustion makes me more vulnerable than I want to allow.

"I'm sure it has nothing to do with your folks flying in today," he says, wryly.

～

Sometime during 7th grade, my family went to visit an old family friend who had recently remarried. During our visit his new wife declared that everyone with AIDS should be put on an island and "that would be that."

This was the world in which I grew up.

This was the world where I came of age and explored my sexuality.

This world told me that being gay was a death sentence and that, for plenty of people, the death sentence was deserved.

When I was in high school in the early 1980s, there were no LGBTQ+ clubs; there were no Rainbow Alliances. It wasn't until I was ten years old that the American Psychological Association declassified homosexuality as a mental disorder. That was 1975. There were no out students; I was called "Ben-Gay" enough to know that coming out was not a viable option.

I perfected the role of the funny, outgoing, asexual, best friend/sidekick and I surrounded myself with mostly girls. Alone, I would walk up and down Columbus Avenue for hours staring into cafés, stealing glances at straight couples with wet, freshly washed hair, imagining their early morning sex, now whispering to one another over coffee and French toast. I longed to experience that kind of intimacy. Once or twice, I dared to go to the West Village where I would wander around Christopher Street, the gay ghetto of New York City. I was terrified of being seen by someone I knew, excited by the sexual energy and confused by it all. Gay men were stuffing their pants with socks—and there was not a gay father to be found.

Returning home, I would lie to my parents about where I had been and wonder what they made of me—always single, surrounded by girls.

The original "don't ask, don't tell."

It was in 1983 that I began to wrestle with the knowledge that I might be attracted to men; AIDS has just been named and fear ran rampant, along with hatred and blame. I internalized my parent's anxiety regarding my sexuality and repressed it even more.

One winter night in 1983, my best friend Lizz and I were in my room doing homework when we were called to dinner. My parents had invited a man I'd never met before. He looked gaunt and fragile. Lizz and I spent most of the dinner huddled at one end of the table, talking. At one point, the man began to cough so violently that all conversation stopped. Lizz and I tried not to giggle.

"That was intense," I said to my parents. The man had just left and we were clearing the table.

My father snapped. "You were rude."

"I'm just saying his coughing fit was crazy," I said, making a what-the-hell face at Lizz.

"He has AIDS, Ben," my mother said.

Her back was to me as she washed some glasses at the sink. Her voice was tight and clipped. It was in this moment that I realized that my parents did wonder about my sexuality. They just wouldn't talk about it.

I avoided Lizz's eyes. I didn't want to know if she suspected it as well.

"We shared food with him," I said, terrified and cornered.

"Isn't it contagious?" Lizz added.

No one knew anything about AIDS.

"Go finish your homework," my mother said sternly.

Once we were back in my room, I wanted nothing more than to confess everything to Lizz: that I was scared, that I felt alone, that I thought I might be gay. But I followed my parents' lead and said nothing. We finished our homework and Lizz went home.

That night, in the darkness of my room, I thought about the dinner guest. Like my parents, I believed that if you were a gay man, you would contract AIDS. The two were synonymous. This stranger was the proof.

In the fall of my senior year, I met James, a junior at Hunter High School. He was preppy but not conservative, radiated warmth, and was wickedly smart. And was out. Intrigued by his self-acceptance and terrified of everything that he represented, I found myself wildly attracted to him. I told no one. I barely admitted it to myself.

Another night, Lizz and I met up with James at a party on the Upper East Side. We made our way through the sprawling apartment and found James with some friends, spread out on the floor of a dimly lit hallway. As soon as I slid down the wall, I was conscious of our legs touching underneath our winter coats. James pressed his leg against mine. Lizz excused herself to get a drink and James put his hand on my thigh. My breathing sped up. Electricity charged through me and my legs began to shake. My throat constricted. James's hand dropped to my inner thigh. I didn't move a muscle. I allowed his hand to remain on my thigh as long I could, then I leapt to my feet. It was more than I could handle. I needed to get away. I was terrified, caught between sexual inexperience and desire. And looming large was the genuine belief that if I allowed myself to be gay I would contract AIDS and die.

"I should check on Lizz," I said, "I'll be right back."

James looked at me with zero judgment and I hated him for his self-assurance, for not calling me out on my bullshit, for allowing me to walk away.

"I'll be here," he said and made a point to rearrange his jacket in order to cover his erection.

"All right," I said, thankful my coat covered my own.

My sexual awakening was new and unlike anything I had ever experienced. It was powerful and alluring and dangerous. I feared it would overtake me.

"Do you want anything while I'm up?" I tried to sound casual.

His eyes dropped to my jacket's placement and he smiled.

"I'm good," I heard him say as I hurried down the hall and back into the crowd.

Several weeks after I ran away from James in the hallway I invited him for a sleepover with Lizz. She had unknowingly become my "beard," before I knew the meaning of the word.

We went out for pizza and watched a movie together in my parents' basement. Eventually we made our way into my sister's old room (she was long gone to college). It had a single bed with a trundle. James and I were in the upper bed and Lizz, who had just fallen asleep, was in the trundle below. I was convinced James could sense my desire but I wondered if he also felt my fear. He placed his hand on my hip and then wrapped it around my chest. My legs trembled. I wanted to respond, to turn around and kiss him but I couldn't; I wouldn't. I was out of bed and on my feet before I knew what happened, even as I felt the disappointment and shame crush my soul.

Unable to meet James's eyes, I told him that I would sleep in the other room, "just to give you more space." Then I scurried away.

2. *Own your sexuality, <u>because</u> it is exhilarating and powerful. And it belongs to you.*

Under the blankets of my other sister's empty bed, I raged at myself. It was the second time I had left James in the lurch and I knew I had ruined it. He was a year younger but light-years ahead of me in his self-acceptance. Alone in the dark, I twisted my thoughts, contorting them to convince myself I was not gay: if I were, I would have turned around and kissed him. If I were gay, I would have stayed in the dimly lit hallway and put my hand on his leg. If I were gay, I wouldn't be so scared. By the time the sun came up, I had convinced myself that I couldn't possibly be gay.

"Hi James," I said, on the phone, later the next day.

"Hey," he replied, doing nothing to hide his exasperation.

I pressed on. "I wanted to thank you," I told him. "I was confused. Thought I might be gay or whatever. But now I know I'm not."

My hollow words fell into the embarrassed silence they deserved.

"So...thanks."

"Okay," he said. "Bye, Ben."

Later I would realize I was wrong about his tone. It was not exasperation. It was pity.

I spent the rest of the day in bed. I never saw James again.

Where would my path have led if I had turned around and kissed James that night? If I had come out earlier would I have still made my way to Daniel? Would Zelda and I have still found one another? I believe your child finds you. But I found her as well.

Tortured by my lies I turned inward and spent more and more afternoons alone in my room or wandering the streets, filling myself up with self-pity and shame. I only went upstairs for dinner. I missed James but would not allow myself to call him. Several weeks passed like this, so I imagine it came as no surprise to my mother when I finally sought her out. It felt like I had nowhere else to turn.

Dinner was over and my homework was finished when I found her alone in her bedroom, folding laundry.

ben barnz

"Hi," I mumbled from the doorway. My throat tightened. I couldn't look her in the eye. "I, um..." I stammered and found it impossible to swallow. It felt as though I were physically shrinking.

"I wonder if I might be gay."

I was met with a deafening silence. I forced myself to look up. Look at me, I thought. See me.

She held a black Rolling Stones t-shirt of mine from their *Tattoo You* tour. It was faded and soft and one of my favorites.

She exhaled slowly.

"I don't think I am," I panicked. "But I wonder sometimes." Two steps forward, one step back.

I wanted her to tell me that everything is as it should be, that my sexuality would not define me. I wanted her to say: gay, straight, whatever, none of it makes any difference to us. Find someone to love. Find someone who will love you back. I wanted her to say that she loved me no matter what. That AIDS was not inevitable. That death and silence were not the only options available to me.

"I don't think you're gay," is what she finally said.

My first thought was to wonder if she would discuss this conversation with my dad.

And my second thought was, if she honestly believed I wasn't gay why did she invite the man with AIDS into our house?

I finished high school without ever dating—a virgin and in deep denial.

In the fall, I set off for Hampshire College, a small liberal arts school in Amherst, Massachusetts, where I promptly fell in love with a sexually open but technically straight man named Danny. Redheaded, brooding, mysterious, he radiated a James Dean vibe. We moved into a four-person apartment our second year. One night we fooled around and awoke to discover his body covered in psychosomatic hives.

During my junior year abroad, I lost my virginity to a girl named Amelia. I was studying acting in London and Amelia, a recent Hampshire graduate, was traveling around Europe with her sister. The three of us spent the day together and the night at a local pub with the unspoken understanding that Amelia and I would be having sex. We eventually made our way back to my ten-by-twenty-foot room with its single bed. We created a makeshift mattress for her sister on the floor where she promptly put on her Walkman and went to sleep. I fumbled around. My first encounter with a woman's body was fast and awkward, made more uncomfortable by the tiny bed and presence of her sister.

In my senior year, I slept with a close friend, Libba. I imagine the sex was fine for her but it was significantly better for me, partly because we were alone in the room.

It was not until my final semester of college that I attended my first gay and lesbian event at college and declared myself bisexual. I am not sure anyone believed or cared about the bisexual part of it.

I graduated from college in 1990. I had never slept with a man.

I moved back into my parents' brownstone where I lived rent-free in one of their upstairs apartments. I was acting at the time and was cast as Demetrius in a production of *A Midsummer Night's Dream*. A week before rehearsals were due to begin, I joined friends who were spending the summer in Provincetown, Massachusetts.

I saw Michael the day I arrived. He worked at a coffee shop at the end of Main Street. He was reed thin, wore a knitted cap, and rode his bike around town as though he owned it. Libba, who was waiting tables in Provincetown, was one of the first friends I told about my attraction to men.

"Take a chance," she said. "You're here for a week. Gay, straight, whatever, go for it."

I hesitated.

"You're asking him out tomorrow, Ben," she declared. "After his shift."

Libba and I followed Michael the next morning as he walked his bike down Main Street. Libba screamed, "Hi!" and nudged me across the street.

Michael turned and smiled at me. "Hi."

I forced my feet to keep moving. "I'm Ben."

"I saw you yesterday," he said. My heart beat faster. "I'm Michael."

He wore a loose-fitted tank top that showed off his smooth upper body and a silver yin-yang symbol on a piece of leather string.

"I wondered if you wanted to have coffee sometime?" I asked, wanting him to say yes and praying he would say no.

"I spend all day with coffee." He had a gentle laugh. "Can I take you to a cool lake instead?" His smile was infectious.

"Sounds great," I managed to say as he climbed on his bike.

"Let's meet at the coffee house at eleven. You'll only need a bathing suit."

"Great," I said, and made my way back across the street where I grabbed Libba's hand. I needed something to hold onto. I had never allowed myself to be this direct with a man and the physical effect was electric.

"I'm proud of you," Libba whispered.

Michael brought me to a lake that was hidden among trees, quiet and secluded. We were the only ones there. It felt as though the place was just waiting for us. The remoteness was liberating: at last I gave myself permission to say yes. And so, at the age of twenty-two, on the shoreline of a small pond in Cape Cod, I had sex with a man. I knew this body and I wanted this body and I knew what it was to pleasure this body. We lay naked in the sun for several hours, dipped repeatedly back into the water and when the sun began to set we made our way back to town. I stayed at his house for the next six nights.

This stranger opened a door that allowed me to understand that I could be both gay and live a fulfilled life. They were not mutually exclusive. AIDS and silence were not my only options.

For the first time I was being honest with myself. Feeling the warm summer sun on my naked body by the side of the lake was real. Michael, freshly showered, saying, "I see you," was real. It was profound. Someone saw me, and more importantly, I finally saw myself.

But a week later, when I returned to my parents' brownstone, I remembered my mother's words: "I don't think you're gay." But this time was different. This time I was determined to hold onto everything that had happened to me in Provincetown. For the first time in my life I compartmentalized. I distanced myself from my family. I excluded my parents from my life, which was unsettling and upsetting because I had always enjoyed being with them. But I had no choice.

I met Steven at the age of twenty-four and began my first long-term relationship. He too was a fellow nester. We hit it off from our first date. A banker, he had a strong jaw line and curly black hair, and he was kind to me. We cooked dinner almost every night, went out to movies and spent a lot of time with his best friend Sarina and her girlfriend. We took turns sleeping at each other's apartments. At my place, I would sneak him past my parents' ground-floor apartment. For the first year of our relationship, I never mentioned him to my family.

I was about to learn that compartmentalized repression inevitably finds an outlet. It has no other choice.

My panic attacks began when I moved to San Francisco in 1991, just before my one-year anniversary with Steven. I was cast as the lead in a play called *Cross-Dressing in the Depression*. I was unmoored in a new town, knew no one, and was surrounded by out gay men; inevitably, my mind turned on itself. The effect was two-fold—it terrified and exhilarated me. The physical sensation from these attacks was one of feeling both fifteen feet tall and smaller than a toddler and I experienced an unwieldy sense of false emotional power. The panic attacks felt similar to my sexual awakening with James, and I welcomed them at first. They felt dangerous and sexy, until one afternoon when they didn't. The attack was upon me so fast that I found myself frozen in the middle of a wide, busy street unable to find my feet, unable to move despite the blaring horns and the echoing shouts: "*Get out of the street...what are you doing?*" I heard the voices around me but I couldn't respond. I have no idea how I managed to move, but I finally did and I ran, non-stop, back to my apartment. My breathing was shallow; I thought I was having a heart attack. Free falling and hysterical, I called Steven. I could hear the fear in his voice. For over three hours, he stayed on the phone with me and eventually eased me into a hot bath where I began to calm down. He remained on the phone with me until he persuaded me to get into bed, insisting that "everything would feel different in the morning." The idea of closing my eyes terrified me. I thought I might not wake up. It was another hour until he lulled me to sleep.

The clock next to the bed read 10:35 AM when I woke up the following morning. I had slept for almost twelve hours. Everything felt absolutely still. And then I thought: Live *your* life; not the one you thought <u>might</u> be.

The morning light filled the room as I sat down at a small wooden writing desk by the large bay window. I had to begin with my parents. It was true that they grew up in a different time and it is also true that the images surrounding us—of AIDS and dying young men and Pride parades with men in leather chaps—left little room to imagine a "normal life." They had to wonder, as I did, what kind of life existed for a gay man at this time. But now I understood that our journeys were not inextricably linked. It was not my responsibility to walk this path with them. My hope was that by taking care of myself I could show us all another way, show us all that another option did exist, show us all that I could create a life with love and children and longevity, just like them.

I took a piece of clean white paper from a short stack on the desk and began to write.

> Dear Mom & Dad,
>
> For a long time there has been a dark cloud over me, something I was trying to fight tooth and nail and because I was shutting off a part of myself, I shut off from a lot of things including you. I now realize that I need to approve and respect myself and a large part of that is coming to terms with the fact that I am bisexual. And right now I am gay. It is stifling growing up constantly being asked, "When are you going to get married?" "What about kids?" But after years of confusion and doubt, of crying myself to sleep because I hated myself for feeling these feelings, for "disappointing" you, finally I have come to terms with it and who I am. And I'm thankful for the fact that I am capable of loving someone else because really that is all that life is about, being able to share your life with another. I won't live in fear anymore. There is so much bad in the world, that if you can find love, that is what matters. And I have. And I want you to know that. I want you to share in that. I want you to know my happiness. I want you to be a part of my life.
>
> It took me years to come to terms with this. I will give you both all the space and time you need. But I couldn't live with myself anymore and not tell you. I have been ashamed, and scared, and self-loathing long enough. It's difficult living in a society that tells you you are wrong, that you don't have the same rights simply because of who you love. It is not a choice. It is simply who I am. I don't know why it is, but it is. I had to take responsibility for <u>my</u> life, for who <u>I</u> am, and this is simply a part of it.
>
> I love you both and I thank you for teaching me about love, and about giving, and about family.

I mailed the letter that day.

A return letter arrived two weeks later.

May 1992

Dearest Ben:

First off, and most important, we love you, we will always love you. Through thick and thin. No matter what. You should know that and be reassured of that. But with love comes responsibility. And we feel a responsibility to advise, criticize, and to challenge. The final decisions and the responsibility for yourself is with you, but we must hope that your decisions will be based on reasoning, not strictly on emotions. That is the sign of maturity; getting beyond solipsism.

As you noted in your letter, the life of a homosexual is not a comfortable life. It is filled with anxieties and biases. We are not quite convinced that your sexual preferences lie there. Why, for example, do you define yourself as bisexual? Are you still confused about it all?

Sex is a funny thing. As you have said, linked to an emotional as well as physical attraction. It involves irrational behavior from rational humans. Control demands a high degree of maturity. A degree too often not achieved.

Do you feel mature enough to decide this is the life, this is the commitment you want to make for the rest of your life? It separates you from the mainstream of life.

The truth is, life is not easy. But it is exciting and it can be fun. But it is not always one or the other. Maturing means understanding all that you have to put up with to achieve some goals you have set.

In life one passes through many stages. Some are inevitable. Some vary with circumstances. It is difficult, if not impossible to understand at a specific stage that you are only passing through and that something more permanent, more mature, will result. The problem lies in separating the emotional involvement in a stage of development from the life that will follow.

We are not trying to talk you out of being "gay." We admit that having a son who is gay is painful and confusing to us. We suffer for his future.

We love you always. We would do anything, sacrifice anything to provide you with happiness. But it is you who must be honest and realistic. Know thyself is easy for me to say, but it must be your charge. We will stand behind you in any decision. We continue to hope and encourage your changing the emphasis on your bisexuality. Meanwhile, now that it's out in the open, let's continue the dialogue.

Love and kisses forever.

It took me some time to write back but I did just before heading back to Manhattan.

July 1992

Dear Mom and Dad,

I'm sorry it has taken me so long to reply to your letter. I needed time to think about it. I found your letter slightly contradictory. I understand that with love comes responsibility to "advise, criticize and <u>challenge;</u>" however, for me it also comes with <u>acceptance</u>. With embracing. This, to me, is a sign of "<u>maturity</u>."

You state throughout your letter that you are not convinced of my sexual preference. Perhaps some of that is my fault, using the terminology "bisexual" seems to have confused you and left you both in a place of uncertainty and questioning. For me it does not. Perhaps I was scared to come right out and say to you that I am gay. Period. No ifs, ands or buts. I said that I am bisexual for you, because I thought that it would be easier for you to deal with. Unfortunately, it left you with the hope on your part that maybe someday I would do the "right" thing and go straight. Get married. But this is my life. That is "maturity."

That is responsibility. To my life.

You said in your letter that the life of a "homosexual is not a comfortable life." To me it is no longer an issue, it is simply a facet. You write asking if "sex is my only driving force?" Is sex your only driving force? Is it Julie's, Andrea's? Why is it that when people think about people of the same sex being together, all they are able to come up with is sex? That love, that companionship, that trust...the same things that make up a "straight" relationship cannot exist?

Please know this—I am happy. I am not harboring a major lie. I am not trying to be something that I am not.

I am being truly honest now, as you requested I be in your letter. "Know thy self" you say. I do. I hope that you will be able to embrace me and love me for who I am and not for who you wished, wish, I will be. You say you will stand behind me in any decision that I make and I hope that is true. Suddenly you have a "gay" son, and how you deal with it concerning the outside world, relatives, friends, strangers making "gay" jokes...suddenly it matters. Because it matters to me. If it still disgusts you, if it still offends you, if it still embarrasses you, it matters. Because people will take their lead off of you. And silence is louder and says more than you could possibly know.

I love you both with all my heart.

I wish I could say I returned to New York and my parents' open arms. But I didn't. Not really. Mainly, there was a silent acceptance. At breakfast one morning, my father told me that he had suggested speaking with me earlier but my mother felt it better that they wait until I come to them. But things were different because I wasn't lying anymore. Steven visited Southampton and I no longer whisked him past my parents' apartment. My middle sister Andrea's response was brilliant and true to character. "Duh," she said, when I came out to her. I reiterated that it mattered to me how they spoke about homosexuality because they now had a gay brother. I joined ACT UP and, despite my resistance to groups, found the unleashed rage empowering. I marched with friends in my Silence = Death t-shirt. It felt like a new chapter, a new beginning. I was ready for it.

~

Ten years later, I am waiting at the LAX baggage claim for my parents to arrive. I feel a sense of pride for how far we have come. They have flown across the country to meet my child and I can't help but smile as I watch them walk toward me, dragging their carry-on bags, their pace quickening to meet their fourth grandchild. The past flashes across my mind: at their dining table, sitting in silence, reading my coming out letter, a magical week the four of us spent in Paris, the two of them blessing us at our commitment ceremony.

You will live many lives within this one long life.

My parents' physical presence calms me. Perhaps time with Zelda might calm their post 9/11 anxiety.

I bend down and kiss Zelda's soft cheek; when I straighten I am engulfed in my mother's arms, then my father's, then I am shoved aside. My mother unstraps Zelda from her car seat and lifts her into her arms.

"She's beautiful, Ben," she says, not taking her eyes off Zelda, whose hair has grown out, tiny golden wisps framing her cherubic face.

"Luckily I had nothing to do with that," I laugh. "How was your flight?"

"Totally fine," my dad states, "like nothing ever happened. Odd." He looks from Zelda to me and smiles, but there is an undercurrent of sadness in his tone.

My mother sits in the back seat next to Zelda. I catch glimpses of her in the mirror as she smiles down at Zelda before she briefly closes her eyes. She works full time as the principal of a public school she founded more than twenty-five years ago, I can sense her exhaustion. I want Zelda to know how extraordinary she is.

When we return home, we have lunch in the backyard with Zelda. Throughout the day, I catch them looking at Zelda and then at me and I know what they are thinking. They want to ask about Liam and Minnesota and the trial but they don't want to discuss it in front of Zelda. When she naps, I drive them to their hotel so they can rest.

"You know I don't nap," my mother says, but we both know

that my father needs one. "Come back in an hour," she insists. "We want every minute we can have with her."

At the end of the day, my mother reads Zelda a bedtime story while my father feeds her a bottle. I put her down to sleep and then join them outside. They have opened a bottle of wine.

"Any updates? On anything?" my mother asks. She can't hide her concern.

"We're talking with our Minnesota lawyer next week," I say. "I have one baby and two lawyers, how crazy is that?" I add in a weak attempt at levity.

Thankfully, my dad picks up on it and adds, "Well, we've had some babies but never a litigator." He smiles at me. "So you beat us there."

They are anxious about Liam and worried for Daniel and me.

Open adoptions did not become widespread until 1982 and my parents, like many of their generation, think of adoptions differently, as awkward transactions fraught with secrecy and shame. And disappointment.

I appreciate that they try to hide their anxiety. They know we are worried enough. With no answers available, we do what parents and grandparents do: we bathe Zelda, take her for walks, cook together, change her diapers, read to her. And so Zelda's family expands.

～

The Tuesday after my parents leave, Daniel, Emma, and I are back at Jonathan's office in another small conference room with fluorescent lighting, this time to meet Nicole Morgan. In her early fifties, she is soft spoken and personable with a slight Southern lilt. She has a legal pad in front of her and two pens. She turns to Daniel and me and says, "I know you have a lot of questions, but right now I must focus on Emma." She exudes confidence.

She has an hour before she appears in court and has many questions. They all focus on Liam, about Emma and Liam, about what Liam did and did not say and when he did or did not say it, about what he did and did not do. She asks time frame questions and personal questions. She is thorough and I have immediate respect for her.

"You two spoke with Scott so that's good," she says as she packs up to leave.

"Yes," we say.

"He's a straight shooter," she says and pushes herself back

from the table. "Emma?" she says, stopping at the door. "Please stay in Los Angeles as long as possible. At least through the Minnesota decision."

Emma looks down at the table, then at Nicole and then again at the table. She can't stay any longer.

Nicole understands this too.

"I realize it's hard, but please at least think about it," Nicole presses.

Emma looks up and meets Nicole's gaze. "I chose the best family I could for Zelda," she states. "Ben and Daniel are her parents and I want to go home."

∼

The following week, Daniel and I drive Emma to the airport. I can feel her excitement; she is a plane ride away from her real life.

At the airport, we drop off two of her cats first. A.J. ran away as she was packing up her apartment, but somehow Emma is at peace with leaving him behind.

"There is so much I want to say," I whisper as I wrap her in my arms. "But...thank you. You changed my life."

For the first time she hugs me a little tighter.

"We will win this fight. You did everything right," I add and look into her eyes. I feel myself about to cry so I step aside. Daniel wraps her in his arms.

She laughs in response to something he says.

"It's weird not being able to walk you to your gate," I say. "I would have liked that."

"A lot has changed," she says.

We stand together for the briefest moment.

Then she turns and walks toward the agent, shows him her ticket and steps onto the escalator.

"We love you," I call out.

She looks over her shoulder as the escalator lifts her up, and she smiles. I wonder if she will ever understand the magnitude of what she has given. It is more than a child. It is the fulfillment of my personal passion. Before we adopted, someone told us that our birthmother would become our biggest hero. Now I truly understood.

We stand there long after she disappears from view.

"She's gone," I finally say.

FROM THE DEPOSITION OF EMMA MURPHY
JANUARY 2002

Q: Let me break it down this way. Did Liam ever tell you that he wanted custody of the child you were carrying?

A: No.

Q: Never at all?

A: No.

Q: So after June 17th, when is the first time that you learned that Liam was actually opposed to any adoption?

A: On September 12th or 13th.

Q: And what is it that you learned that day?

A: That he had—his sister had e-mailed Jonathan Ross and said they were trying to stop the adoption.

Q: At the end of your conversation with Liam on June 17th did you feel he was on board with the adoption plans?

A: I didn't feel he was on board, but he said—if—I believe, if that was best, he did—he wasn't going to do anything to stop it.

Q: How did you feel when you were pregnant?

A: Scared.

13

A plane roars overhead as Daniel maneuvers the car out of the airport and onto the freeway.

"It *was* strange," Daniel says, "not being able to walk her to the gate."

I roll down my window and allow the early fall breeze to fill the car. The cool air is a relief.

In a few hours Emma will be home, in her own place, surrounded by the life she knows, and I felt relief. Now if we could only get the court in Minnesota to assign us a judge.

"Remember when we picked her up for the first time?" Daniel adds as he glances over at me and laughs. "You went through like a hundred outfits."

"Maybe not that casual," Daniel jokes as he stands in the doorway of our room. He has just returned from a morning run and sweat drips off him. I am in a pair of boxers and a t-shirt; clothes are spread out all over the bed.

In an hour we will get in the car to pick up Emma at the airport. In an hour we will meet our birthmother for the first time. In an hour nothing will be the same.

"You're so funny!" I snap, though I know he is teasing. "I don't know what to wear. It seems important somehow, first impressions and all that."

"Keep it simple," he says and drops his wet shirt into the hamper before he heads off to the shower.

"Keep it simple," I repeat, irritated by his calm demeanor.

Sadie begins to bark loudly in the backyard and Daniel shouts at her.

"Sadie! Stop barking!"

And like that, I feel better. He isn't so calm. How could he be? A stranger hurtles toward us at five hundred miles per hour carrying our child. Once she lands, Daniel and I will no longer be just a couple ever again. Once her plane touches ground our relationship will forever be altered.

I force myself to concentrate on this stranger, on Emma. She must be terrified. I think about the ability to trust, to choose hope instead of doubt, and it hits me: if we are going to make it through this experience intact we have to trust one another.

Daniel is right, keep it simple. I grab my favorite pair of jeans and leave the choice of a shirt for later. One of the tricky things about being in a gay relationship is keeping our looks separate, not too matchy-matchy. One of us can choose a sweater so as not to match the other's button-down, or a pair of jeans instead of khakis, but that is about the best we can do.

Ravenously hungry, I cross the hall and enter the kitchen. Emma's plane is scheduled to land in two hours. I have been tracking it since it took off. Daniel and I have jobs, pay our bills, own a house—but this is Next Level, this is *adult*. We are in charge of this situation—no one else.

Get it together, I think.

Keep it simple.

I grind coffee beans and pour water into the machine. I wander into the dining room and pick up *The New York Times* Daniel has left on the table. I glance at the headlines but I'm too distracted to understand them, so I drop the newspaper back onto the table and walk back into the kitchen. Daniel stands in front of the coffee machine with a mischievous grin on his face.

"Were you waiting to turn this on?" he asks.

"Piss off," I say and push him out of the way. "Be gentle. I am close to the edge."

"Maybe you should get a massage?" he jokes. "Or we could go see a movie?"

"All excellent ideas," I say, "But let's say we drive out to the airport and meet the woman carrying our baby."

"I like it!" he says.

My hunger vanishes and the thought of food makes me sick. I want to shout from the rooftop and tell anyone within earshot that we are about to have a baby, but it is too soon for that, so instead we do what we would do on any given morning—we make the bed and drink our coffee.

But this morning is not any other morning. This morning changes everything.

Twenty minutes later Daniel pushes his chair back from the table and says, "Get dressed. We should go."

I choose a dark-blue, short-sleeved button down shirt as Daniel has claimed the black jeans and a faded green polo. We put Sadie out in the yard and lock the front door.

"Things are going to be different when we return to this house," I say as he backs out of the driveway.

"Very," he agrees.

Traffic is light and we arrive at the airport with time to spare. We park the car and make our way to her gate, which is fairly empty.

"Should we have brought her something? Some flowers, maybe?" I ask as we find seats near a large glass window overlooking the tarmac.

"You think? That seems awkward."

"You're right. She's not a contestant on a game show." I stand up. I can't sit still. "Do we hug her? We should hug her." Daniel looks at me. "Maybe that's too much? Too intimate?" I can't stop talking.

"No, it's good. We should hug her," Daniel says.

"Jesus. What must she be thinking now?"

Daniel shrugs. "Relief, I hope."

I sit back down. We fall into silence. So many thoughts running through my mind: who is this woman? What does she look like? Is she having a boy or a girl? Do I care? What will it be like to parent with Daniel? Have we discussed this enough? Might she change her mind after the baby is born? Will she like us?

A plane pulls up to the gate.

"She's here," I say to myself and press my hand to the window.

Daniel joins me.

"What if we don't recognize her?" Daniel asks. "I mean we've only seen a grainy fax of her driver's license."

An agent opens the door.

"We'll keep our eyes peeled for the blonde, pregnant woman who looks scared out of her mind."

There is a garbled announcement about the baggage claim carousel and a delayed connection to San Jose.

"You're standing too close," I whisper.

"What?"

"You're standing too close. Move back."

He looks at me for a moment. "Really?"

"Yes, give her space."

He steps back, which allows a balding, middle-aged man to slip in and take his place. "Better?"

"Yes. Give us a moment to take each other in."

A trickle of people emerges from the walkway, then nothing. Those of us still waiting take a collective step forward.

Despite the fact that Emma's driver's license listed her height (5'6") and weight (120), I find myself looking for a heavy woman; otherwise, how is she *just* starting to show?

Then she walks out and everything starts to unfold very slowly, and also very quickly.

Is this the moment I lost control of time?

Her beauty takes me by surprise. Her long blond hair frames her oval face. Her eyes are green. She wears a loose-fitting t-shirt and now I understand why it's hard to tell she is pregnant: her swollen breasts allow her shirt to hang loosely over her stomach. For a split second, I wonder if I am looking at the wrong woman until she raises her hand and gives a small wave.

Of course she knows what we look like; we sent her our book full of photos.

Of course she is relieved.

Of course we should hug her, I think, as I wrap my arms around her.

I swear I feel a weight lift from her shoulders. She is no longer alone. Or perhaps the relief is mine.

"Welcome to California," I say and step back.

"Thanks," she says quietly.

24. It is important how things begin.

Daniel hugs her.

"You must be so tired. You've been up since five this morning, right?"

"Yeah and yes, I am," she says. I appreciate her honesty.

"Let's get your bags," Daniel says.

"And your cats," I add.

We walk toward baggage claim and I trail a couple of steps behind. I want to record this moment in my mind, the first time I see our child's biological mother. Her physical presence makes everything vivid and real, which is both terrifying and breathtaking.

The wait for her bags feels interminable, the small talk excruciating. She is spent, we are all out of our element, and ultimately we are strangers. Strangers with a massive, intimate experience, which has only just begun.

This is not going to be easy.

Her bags arrive and we head off to retrieve her cats.

We park just outside an enormous cargo hold not far from the terminal. The hangar looms before us like something out of a sinister sci-fi movie. Inside does not disappoint: it is dark and vast and empty and freezing cold. I can tell Emma is overwhelmed and exhausted. She wants to see her cats, something she knows, something she loves. She doesn't move.

We are the parents. We must take charge.

"Hi," Daniel says to the woman working behind the counter. "We're picking up three cats. Murphy." He turns around and smiles at Emma.

"Wait here," the woman says and then speaks into a walkie-talkie, "Murphy pick-up."

Something about her tone is off. Daniel and I catch each other's eyes.

"They'll be right out," she says with definite hesitation.

"You must be excited to see them?" I say to Emma, choosing to ignore my uneasiness; I pray her cats aren't dead.

"They've never flown before," she says nervously. "I hope they're all right."

Then everything happens at once.

"I'm sure they're fine," I say just as the pungent stench of cat shit fills the air. The woman behind the counter says, "It seems one of your cats had an accident."

There are two cats in one crate; the other is alone. The woman attempts to step away from the smell, but there is no escaping it. Daniel and I avoid looking at one another.

The day moves from the surreal to the absurd.

No one speaks as the woman pushes the paperwork across the counter. Daniel signs it and slides it back. We all nod at one another and step out of the hangar grateful for the fresh air. Emma looks as though she might cry.

Thankfully, the cat that flew alone is the one who shat himself. I count this as a blessing. It could have been twice as bad.

"There is a pet store on our way to your apartment," I tell Emma as we place the cats as far back in the car as possible. "We'll get him cleaned right up."

"I feel bad," she says.

This is not how any of us wanted to begin. And we awkwardly comfort her.

"He'll be like new," Daniel says.

We pull out of the lot and roll down every window.

I recall something about cat shit and pregnant women: pregnant women are not supposed to handle cat shit, but can smell it; or, they are not supposed to smell it, but can touch it? I can't remember. I try not to panic. I think about throwing the cat out the window to protect our child.

Despite the air, the smell is unbearable. I can't breathe.

"Sweet Mother of God!" I blurt and add a quick laugh. Daniel glares at me. I turn around and hope for a conspiratorial smile but Emma gives no indication she even heard me.

"After we drop your cat off we'll show you your place and give you some time to settle in," I say, hoping to give her something else to think about.

We come to a stop at a red light heading north on La Cienega Boulevard. A massive black Escalade pulls up alongside our car. I glance out the window and see a hipster with a shaved head, goatee and inked right arm. He grins at me and gives a s'up head nod.

"Oh!" I let out as I realize that the guy is getting a blowjob. The guy has one hand on the wheel while the other rests on top of the head of a blond woman.

Daniel looks at me and I direct him with my eyes to the Escalade.

Never has a red light taken so long to change.

Welcome to Los Angeles.

I feel my level of panic rise from the collective anxiety, from the smell of cat shit, from the blowjob in the car next to us. In my oxygen-deprived mind, I convince myself that Emma will decide Los Angeles is an unfit place for her child to grow up. She will insist that we turn the car around and drive her and her shit-covered cat back to the airport.

"Look!" I say, too loudly. "Look out the window!" I turn around and make sure Emma knows I am pointing, *away* from the man and his Escalade. "Do you see that building?" I say, making it up as I go along. "That ugly gray one? I...um...worked there for like two days," I lie. "Remember, Daniel? Remember when I worked there?" I laugh awkwardly and hope Daniel will continue the ruse and keep Emma distracted. His eyes are as wide as saucers.

"I remember that. You hated that job," he adds, his voice much higher than normal.

The light finally turns green. We have kept her attention away from the Escalade though she probably now considers us very odd. Daniel steps on the gas but not before the man gives me a thumbs up.

When Daniel pulls up to Petco, I jump at the chance to take the cat inside and give myself a moment to regroup.

Ten more minutes and we pull up to the guard booth at Park LaBrea, a gated community with multiple apartment buildings, located in central Los Angeles. We have rented Emma an apartment here; this will be her home for the next two months.

"We are here to meet Sarah," I tell the guard.

Sarah runs the Park LaBrea rental office, I found her phone manner brusque when we spoke a week earlier, so I am anxious about meeting her in person. I would prefer this morning didn't become any more uncomfortable.

When we meet Sarah, she is pleasant and personable. She is also well over six feet tall.

"You must be Emma. Welcome to L.A.," she says, offering Emma her hand. "I just need you to sign some forms."

Emma smiles. She keeps her eyes down, crosses her legs. It looks as though she is trying to take up as little space as possible.

We had asked Sarah not to list the amount of the rental in the agreement. The economics of adoption are wildly complicated: we want Emma to know we can care for a child but we don't want to rub our (comparative) wealth in her face. We didn't want Emma to think we threw money around.

But there it was: $1600 a month, repeated multiple times. But all Emma wants is to be in her apartment, alone. I can feel it. She signs her name without reading a word and we leave.

I take hold of Daniel's arm as Emma enters the apartment. I want her to have a moment to take it in on her own. We set everything up in advance of her arrival, and tried to make it feel as homey as possible.

It is a large studio apartment, with wood floors and windows that look out on green shrubs.

She walks slowly behind the couch and allows her hand to brush the throw we draped over the back. She takes in the two tall stacks of DVDs that sit next to the television. Her back is to us so we can't read her expression. She looks over at the double bed covered with a patchwork quilt and the handful of colorful throw pillows we put at the head. As she heads for the bathroom she reaches down and touches the blanket we draped at the foot of her bed.

She is tactile, I think.

We place her bags next to the sofa.

She walks into the bathroom with a white terry cloth bathrobe and a folded set of bath towels.

"It's nice," she says quietly as she passes us on her way to the kitchen. We stocked the refrigerator with fresh juices, cold cuts, fruits and vegetables. Several choices of cereal sit on the countertop.

She notices the litter box and the cat food.

We had also left a fresh bouquet of flowers on the dining table with a few toys for her cats.

"Thanks," she says as she picks up a toy and twirls it in her hand.

"We'll give you some time to settle in and then come back around 3:30."

"Sure," she says as she sits down on the couch, unlatching the cat crate.

"We'll pick up A.J. before we come get you."

"And you are going to love Dr. Davis," Daniel adds.

"Please let us know what's missing foodwise and I can pick it up for you tomorrow," I add as we make our way to the door.

She smiles as she watches her cats poke their heads out of the crate, her attention fixed on them.

"You have my cell number, right?" I ask.

"Yes."

And we are out the door.

"Holy shit," I declare, falling into the car. "This is going to be exhausting!"

"She doesn't talk much," Daniel says. "Though to be fair she has been up since five this morning and her cat did shit itself."

Daniel and I finally erupt with laughter, partly because of her poor cat but mostly because of our own pent-up anxiety.

We pull out of Park LaBrea and onto Beverly Boulevard.

"She's lovely," he says.

"And sweet. And really pretty."

Neither of us says it but what parent doesn't harbor a secret, superficial desire to have a beautiful child?

"She really doesn't look pregnant, does she?"

"Not really, no."

For a while we drive in silence, each of us processing the morning's events.

"Is it bad that we're making her see Dr. Davis today?"

"Maybe," Daniel says, "but we need to have her checked out. Especially since she hasn't seen a doctor yet."

It's hard not to feel bad. Emma is exhausted and overwhelmed and in an hour a stranger will poke and prod her. On the one hand we want her to feel safe, that she can trust us, that we are her confidants. On the other hand we are businessmen insuring our investment.

Two hours later the three of us are back in the car on our way to meet our gynecologist.

"Is everything all right at your place? Do you need anything?" I ask.

"No. I'm good."

"The cats settled in?" Daniel asks.

"Yes. Thanks."

Silence. My need for her to like us strangles me.

"You're going to really like Dr. Davis," I say in an attempt to fill the void, then I remember Daniel said that exact sentence a few hours earlier in her apartment.

Get it together, I think.

"He works out of Good Samaritan Hospital," I decide to add. "Close to downtown."

Stop.

We drive in silence.

Dr. Davis's reception area has two sofas which frame a rectangular coffee table scattered with magazines. Most are weekly gossip magazines but there are a few parenting magazines. I wonder if they will make Emma self-conscious or if she even notices them. The receptionist gives Emma a stack of forms to fill out. Daniel and I flip through magazines while she checks off boxes and signs her name several times.

Two men and a birthmother.

I drop one magazine on the table and pick up another.

Emma has never seen a doctor.

What if we discover some sort of complication, some birth defect? What would we do? Would we say, "Thank you, but no thank you," and send Emma home? I couldn't do that—and yet.

I feel ashamed.

Now convinced something is seriously wrong with Emma's baby, I look over at Daniel. He meets my panicked stare with a questioning look, but before I can whisper anything, Dr. Davis appears.

"You must be Emma," he says with a warm smile on his face. Tall and lanky with receding hair and big ears, he gives off an air of calm and warmth.

"Yes," she answers.

"It's a pleasure to meet you. Let's you and I go sit together and then we'll bring the guys in."

I am brought back to our initial meeting with him two weeks earlier.

～

We first spoke with Dr. Davis the day after Emma told us she wanted us to adopt her child. We find ourselves having to come out again and again—something we haven't had to do for years: first to Jonathan Ross, then Sarah at Park LaBrea, now to Dr. Davis.

"I can make time tomorrow afternoon if you and Daniel would like to come meet me and see the hospital," he had said.

Dr. Davis works in a white brick building that overlooks Wilshire Boulevard—I had driven by it many times; suddenly this building matters, matters a lot. We take the elevator up to the third floor. A young nurse takes our names, apparently unfazed by two men meeting with a gynecologist; her nonchalance makes me giddy. We join two visibly pregnant women in the waiting area.

Every step we take confirms what I understand intellectually but haven't processed emotionally: this is actually happening. I unconsciously giggle and both women stare at me; one seems amused, the other not.

Feeling defensive, I furrow my brow at Ms. Un-Amused and think: *where's your husband?* Then I feel bad.

"Excuse me," the nurse says. Daniel gets up from the couch to speak with her.

"Do you have your insurance card?" I hear her ask.

We had wondered about this. Would insurance cover a gynecologist for a man? Daniel returns to the couch and informs me that we are, in fact, not covered and all expenses related to the birth will come out of pocket. Before I am able to calculate what these expenses might be, Dr. Davis stands before us, hand outstretched.

"It is a pleasure to meet you both," he says.

He leads us down a short hallway, covered floor to ceiling with baby photos and thank you notes. Will our child's photograph be on his wall one day?

We follow him into his office and sit down across from him. "How exciting for you guys. Tell me what's going on and where you are in the process."

"Well," I say, diving in, "we're adopting a baby and the birthmother is seven months pregnant and coming to L.A. at the end of the week. She hasn't seen a doctor yet so that's a concern." I am talking too fast and can't stop. "And our friend Julia worked with you during a home birth and could not have spoken more highly of you."

"This is all new for us," Daniel jumps in, to slow me down. "We were hoping we could ask you some questions and perhaps you could fill us in on what else we might need to know."

"Great," says Dr. Davis. "Why don't I show you our maternity ward and you can ask questions as we go?"

He leads us through what looks like a service entrance to another elevator, which opens onto the maternity ward. The hushed quiet surprises me. Dr. Davis introduces us to the nurse staff on duty—again, a coming out—and once again the response is unfazed. I realize how much of my own childhood homophobia I still carry inside of me. Not a single nurse cares about our sexuality.

The rooms are large and airy with dark mahogany, wide-wood

planked floors and private bathrooms; some even offer birthing tubs. I feel my pulse quicken as this experience becomes more and more of a reality.

We ask questions. Dr. Davis never makes us feel as if he needs to be anywhere but with us, right now.

Yes, he has handled adoptions and birthmothers before.

Yes, he has handled same-sex adoptions before.

Yes, his hospital and nurse staff members have also handled adoptions.

Back in his office, we show him the blood work Jonathan Ross requires. We emphasize that we never want Emma to feel any pressure from us, she should have whatever kind of birth she wants. Dr. Davis assures us her decisions will be respected. He thoughtfully suggests placing Emma on another floor after the birth so she won't be surrounded by the sound of newborn babies.

"I would like to see her as soon as she arrives in Los Angeles," he says as we make our way back toward the reception area. "I want to build a relationship. Normally I would have had months already."

We schedule Emma's first appointment for the day she arrives.

"Thank you so much," Daniel says and shakes his hand.

"Yes, and for your time," I add as we step into the elevator.

"I am excited for you guys," we hear him say as the doors close.

"I love my gynecologist," I shout up to the sky as soon as we are outside.

∿

Two weeks later we are back in the waiting room and Emma is with Dr. Davis.

"What if something is wrong with the baby?" I whisper to Daniel.

"What?" His head snaps toward me. He looks irritated.

"I mean Emma's never been seen by a doctor or taken any prenatal vitamins. Do you think you are ready to raise a child with Down syndrome?"

"What the fuck, Ben?" Daniel says, trying to manage his own anxiety.

"I don't think I would handle it very well. I mean, I suppose I would. I mean I wouldn't turn her away. But...."

"Ben. Stop. You're spinning."

A moment later Dr. Davis appears.

"Why don't you come back to my office?"

There is something in his tone which confirms my worst fears. I look at Daniel as if to say, *see?* Daniel shakes his head.

"Emma will join us in a minute, she's just changing her clothes," Dr. Davis says as we follow him back down the baby photo hallway. I wonder if Emma imagined her child's photo up on these walls.

"I wanted to talk to you before bringing her in."

I grow hot, convinced bad news is coming. It takes forever before he gets out the rest of his sentence.

"Everything looks great. The baby and Emma are both healthy and strong," he says as he closes the door.

You are healthy.

I finally exhale. Daniel looks at me pointedly.

After almost twenty years of imagining this moment, wanting this moment, praying for this moment, it has arrived. I sit across the table from a doctor who tells me, the expectant father, that the baby is healthy.

"That's great," I say. "Great." I can't stop smiling.

"Emma does seem detached from the baby," he continues, "which to a degree is expected in this situation. But she is definitely detached. Hard to say one hundred percent if this is a good thing or not but for now I would lean toward good. She certainly seems clear about her decision."

Daniel looks at me: *stay calm.*

"I spoke with her about the birth and the one thing she is certain about is not wanting to feel any pain."

"Seems about right to me," I laugh.

If I were placing my child for adoption, I would want to be detached. If I were giving birth, I would want to feel as little pain as possible. I like Emma more and more.

Dr. Davis smiles.

"I'd like to see her once a week until the birth. It's more than I would normally see someone this far along but since I did not have the first seven and half months, I'd like that time now."

"Great," Daniel and I say simultaneously.

"Would you like to know the sex?" he asks expectantly.

"No," we say in unison and are greeted by a look of surprise.

We too found the need to detach. Knowing the sex of the child made us vulnerable. If Emma changes her mind, a genderless baby might allow us some emotional wiggle room.

There is a gentle knock on the door and Emma enters. She sits close to the door.

"I let them know everything is well," Dr. Davis says to Emma, who looks relieved and exhausted. "I'd like to see you once a week and I'm going to give you some vitamins, okay?"

"Okay." She smiles. She is as won over by his gentleness as we were.

"I have to be honest with you though, the vitamins taste terrible," he laughs. "But I need you to take them," he adds firmly. "And the guys have decided not to find out the sex of the baby."

There is a penetrating silence and I worry that we've disappointed her. But there is no way to explain our reasoning to her.

"I'll see you in a week," he says as he stands up, giving Emma a hug.

In the elevator Emma says, "You were right. He's nice."

"The nicest, right?" I say as we descend back down to the lobby.

"Wow. These are really big!" Emma exclaims as she peers into the jar of vitamins in her hand.

"Really? Let me see," I say as we pile back into the car.

They are large, bigger than the biggest multi-vitamin I have ever forced down my throat. I feel guilty. But I also want her to take the vitamins.

"Sorry?" I offer, unsure what else to say.

We head back to her apartment, talking only a little, mostly about her cats. So many questions race through my mind: How are you feeling? What is it like to have a baby grow inside of you? Are you happy here? Do you like us? Do you feel safe? But I can't— not yet—probably not ever.

She opens her door as soon as we pull up to her apartment. She has only been here for six hours. Two months seems endless.

"We'll be back in about two hours with dinner. Do you like Chinese food?"

"Sure," she says. "And thanks."

We want to celebrate her arrival, her choice, her gift, and the best way we know to do that is with food.

We wait to drive away until she walks into her building.

"The baby's fine," I say as I pull away.

When we return with dinner two hours later, Emma is on the couch, watching a basketball game.

"You like basketball?" I ask.

"I do," she says, "and football. I like watching sports."

Daniel and I stand behind the couch and watch for a minute with two large bags of Chinese food in our hands. Daniel and I have an entire wordless conversation:

Me: Could we be *more* gay right now?

Daniel smiles.

Me: What do we do?

Daniel: I want to eat at the table.

Me: But she seems happy.

Daniel: Table.

Me: You're right.

"Hope you're hungry," I say unpacking the food.

"We brought lots of it," Daniel adds and begins to remove one container after another from his bag. The small table overflows with takeout containers and more bundled napkins and chopsticks than there are people. I grab plates and glasses of water from the kitchen as she turns off the game and joins us at the table.

"Do you like moo shoo pork?" I ask. "It's one of my favorites."

"I've never had it before," she responds without a hint of self-consciousness.

I see her eyes scan the table. I leap up to grab some forks from the kitchen.

She takes a fork and I decide to follow suit.

"Do you like it?" I ask.

Daniel looks at me: *Relax.*

"It's good," she says.

Daniel raises his glass of water. "We are so happy you are here and we feel very blessed that you came into our lives."

She lifts her glass but keeps her gaze down.

"We think you are amazing," I add.

We eat quickly.

I clean up and leave the leftovers in the fridge.

"I'll give you a call in the morning. Daniel has some meetings but you and I can go do something. But let's see how you're feeling," I add, wanting to give her an out.

Daniel takes out his wallet as I tie up the garbage.

"You don't need to do that," she insists. It is an uncomfortable moment. Technically, we are not meant to exchange any money; it's illegal to buy or sell babies. But this is different. She has no income while she is here, and if she does want to go out, we don't want her to spend her own money.

"We want to," Daniel insists and hands her fifty dollars. "Just in case. Get some rest."

She folds the money in her hand.

"And if you need anything, no matter what time, just call us."

"I will," she says. She is ready to be left alone.

We get home and collapse in front of the television, channel surfing until we land on the beginning of *Fight Club*. We watch grown men beat the shit out of each other—a perfectly surreal ending to a perfectly surreal day.

At eleven, we crawl into bed. I think about Emma, alone in a new city having just met the people she chose to raise her child.

As I drift off I wonder: when does the baby go from being hers to ours?

14

October flies by with no developments in the case.

On Halloween we put Zelda in a bumblebee onesie. We take a photograph of the three of us on our front step. Daniel and I could not look happier. Zelda looks bewildered. While I set up bowls of candy for trick-or-treaters, Daniel downloads the digital pictures on his computer and emails them to our family. My mother responds immediately and declares her, "THE cutest bumblebee" she has ever seen. Then she adds, "She'd be even cuter *here* with all of her cousins!"

Children come knocking, we give out candy in fistfuls and neighbors admire Zelda. At 6:30 we turn off our porch light and curl up on our bed, reading to Zelda while she devours her bedtime bottle.

My attachment to her grows deeper every day. My life before her feels more and more distant.

In early November, Scott Foster calls from Minnesota.

"I can only imagine how hard this all is," he says, "living with this level of uncertainty. But please know I am doing everything in my power to help you keep your child."

He tells us that he requested a new judge. The initial judge assigned to our case is known to be "pro-birthfather."

I had no idea one could request a different judge. Couldn't this go on forever, each side asking for different judges? I don't ask. I don't want the answer to be yes.

The following morning, I take Zelda to her two-month check-up. While I wait for the pediatrician, I lay her on the "meat" scale to see how much she weighs. If I factor in the initial adoption costs, the medical expenses, and the additional litigation fees, how much would Zelda be worth by the pound?

After her examination, her doctor announces that, "She is doing beautifully. She's even holding her head up on her own."

I feel pride, unearned but I savor it.

Q: When did you and Emma first start dating?

A: Sometime in November.

Q: For how long?

A: Couple of months.

Q: Did you ever live together?

A: No.

Q: How often did you see her?

A: Quite often. Probably four, five times a week.

Q: Did you ever meet her parents?

A: Once I met her mother.

Q: Did you know where her mother lived?

A: Yeah.

15

A week later, I wake up alone. Once again, Daniel snuck Zelda out.

It's chilly and I don't want to leave the warmth of our bed. I pull the quilt more tightly around myself. I think about Emma and try to imagine her life in Minnesota—her home life, her apartment, her family. Most of it I make up; she shared very little with us. Once she referred to the main road in town where everyone hung out; I am only able to picture it in some stereotypical *Footloose* kind of way. What is it like for her to harbor this decision? Is she haunted by an ever-present fear of her parents finding out? Does she ever want to tell them?

Emma's departure is harder for me then I imagined. I think about reaching out, checking in on her, but I also must allow her to move forward on her own. In the end, I am not her parent.

As much as I appreciate the quiet, it proves impossible to turn off my Zelda-radar. I wonder if that ever goes away, listening for your child.

When I leave our room, I realize Daniel must have taken her and Sadie for a walk. I head out onto the patio with my computer.

For a few moments, no one needs anything from me. I can't remember the last time this was true. The sun feels good in the cool November air. I warm my hands on a cup of tea and button up the heavy grey cardigan Daniel gave me for my birthday.

The phone rings and my heart lurches. But it is only my parents calling to check in. They want to know when I am going to move back "home" with their grandchild.

"Her cousins keep asking," my mother claims.

I laugh it off though I feel the pull of family differently now. My parents have wanted me to move back east ever since I left New York nine years ago.

∾

I met Daniel in January 1994, after I had been in Los Angeles for just over a year.

He was completing his final year at USC Film School. I auditioned for his thesis film, *Gasp*. Though the audition was arranged through my agent, the fact that we were to meet at his house gave me pause. When I pulled up in front of his house, I saw him on the phone outside his front door in a multi-colored baseball cap and pleated shorts. He looked like he was twelve years old. I considered calling my agent to tell her I had come down with the flu. But I glanced around my old VW Bug and decided that work begets work. I grabbed my picture and resume and stepped out of my car.

Where would I be today if I had driven away? Would you and I have still found one another?

Daniel opened the door and my first words to him (which he never forgot) were, "Hi, I'm Ben. It's nice to meet you. I have to pee."

We sat in his living room and read scenes together. He was smart and charming. An hour later, when I returned to my car, I wanted the role. The following day he cast me. Over the next six months I became a member of his tight-knit circle of friends.

He got a job at the restaurant where I worked, a mediocre, vegan restaurant in Santa Monica. Neither one of us lived anywhere close to the restaurant nor was it a particularly popular restaurant. At the end of our shift we were often left with as little as twenty-five dollars in our pockets. But we were together.

It was during our slow shifts together that I realized how intelligent he was, where we discussed our families and marveled at their similarities; it was here that I discovered that he and his boyfriend were having problems and heading toward a breakup. It was here that I allowed myself to notice his smooth forearms which I quickly found every conceivable excuse to touch.

It was here that I realized I was in love with him.

Seven months after we met, Daniel asked if we might go out for a drink. In a crowded bar on Beverly Boulevard, he told me that he had "feelings for me." I played it cool. I did not want to be responsible for anyone's breakup.

"It's important how things begin," I told him.

He understood. He needed to end his current relationship before we could even think of moving forward.

A couple of months later, he moved out of the house he shared with his boyfriend. We started dating the next day. A year later, we moved into a one-bedroom house in Laurel Canyon. The house was small. But it was ours. The living room had large, glass-paned windows, which looked out over Laurel Canyon, low ceilings and a fireplace. The L-shaped kitchen felt like it belonged in a studio apartment in New York City. It connected the living room and a sunroom where we ate all of our meals. Our bedroom was upstairs next to the one, tiny bathroom. We had to step into the shower stall because it was also a sitting tub. We bought our first expensive piece of furniture, a shabby-chic over-sized white armchair; we hung up what art we had and bought a pullout sofa for the living room. Six months later we drove to Riverside to choose a puppy from an eight-week-old litter. The ranch was strewn with cigarette butts, all the puppies gamboled in a large shady area covered by trees. The runt leapt onto my chest and licked my face. I could not get enough of her sweet breath and an hour later we drove her home, only then realizing that our puppy chose us.

Today, when someone asks Daniel and me how long we have been together, we pause.

I have been with him close to half my life.

Every night we switch sides of the bed. In our nighttime ritual, we trade our books and water glasses. We do this so that when one of us dies we won't mourn "his" side of the bed.

When we are out to dinner, we switch plates halfway through; I can't recall the last time I ate my own dinner. At home, one of us will make dinner and the other will clean up. I pick out the friend's birthday gift while he writes the card and for the nights we remember to have Shabbat dinner, I make the challah and he says the prayers.

16

I feel alone.

Caring for a baby is isolating; now it is compounded by the dread and fear, the sensation that something lurks just beyond, something irrevocable. Daniel and I share our fears less and less.

Zelda finishes her 2 AM bottle. When I lay her down on her bed, Sadie groans as she stretches. They choose us, I think. They choose us.

All I long for is a deep night's sleep. But I can't, so I wander the house in the dark.

Two more weeks have passed and still we wait. Wait to hear about a new judge. Wait to hear about our trial. Wait on a decision about jurisdiction. Wait to be told what we know: that Zelda is our daughter. We hold on to that truth with every ounce of strength we have.

In the living room, a blue light seeps through the white curtains, but when I pull them open it is only the light from a flickering streetlamp. Across the street, I spy a woman sitting in her living room, alone. She looks nothing like Emma, but something in the way she looks down reminds me of her.

⁓

A week after Emma arrives, we stroll through the aisles of Kmart, looking for maternity clothes. She still looks only three months pregnant. It is summer and very warm—too warm.

We are surrounded by racks of maternity clothes. Emma glances this way and that. "Do you mind if we look at the regular clothes?" she asks. "I hate maternity clothes. I bet I can just buy clothes that are bigger."

Forty-five minutes later we stand in line at the register with two pairs of elastic waistband jeans and some shirts.

"You sure you don't want to look around a little more?"

"I'm kind of tired," she says.

"Oh. Of course."

I worry this is a referendum on me, then I remember she is almost eight months pregnant, she is exhausted, and we don't have that much to talk about yet. But we will.

While I take my credit card out, she quietly says, "I don't really like how I look pregnant."

Now I understand her reticence.

"You look beautiful," I insist.

"Yeah, no."

Standing in Kmart, it hits me. Our experiences of this same event are fundamentally different. Daniel and I believe that what is happening is the very definition of a miracle. Emma wants to get through it. She wants to get back to the life she knew.

The next time I see Emma, I am astounded by the change in her body.

Three days later and she suddenly looks eight months pregnant.

She is beautiful. But I say nothing.

We decided to see a movie, which suits me just fine. It constitutes an outing but we don't need to worry about keeping the conversation alive. The lights dim as we enter the movie theater and the previews begin.

"*Boys were her destiny. Boys were her weakness,*" the voice booms into the darkness of the theater.

"Mom? Pop?" Drew Barrymore says, "I'm pregnant." The narrator continues: "*From director Penny Marshall comes the story of a girl whose dreams took an unexpected turn.*"

Are you fucking kidding me?

Popcorn falls out of my hand and onto the floor.

"*Experience the plans we make, the risks we take, and the people in our lives who make it worth the ride. Riding in cars with boys. Based on a true story.*"

I don't move a muscle. I have no idea what Emma's reaction is. We don't know one another well enough to laugh about it. After the movie, I drive her home. Neither of us acknowledges the preview.

Sometime around early August, I take Emma to meet with her Adoption Service Provider, Anne Brody.

Anne's job is to make a comprehensive assessment of Emma's commitment to the adoption plan, while ensuring that she is fully aware of her rights and options throughout the adoption process. The law requires Emma to sit down with Anne at least once to discuss the adoption placement.

The interior of Anne's office building is as gray and dull as the milky-beige of the stucco exterior. Eerily devoid of life, a ghostly quality permeates the silent hallway. I can feel Emma's desire to bolt and I don't blame her. We sit down on the folding chairs outside Anne's office and wait.

"This place gives me the creeps," Emma says.

Anne's door opens and now another six-foot-tall woman with a lean runner's build greets us. Her ill-fitting corporate clothing is at odds with her warm and engaging demeanor. She focuses her attention squarely on Emma.

"Welcome to Los Angeles, Emma," Anne says and shakes her hand. "I'm Anne." She then turns to me and laughs, "Which one are you?"

I like her.

"I'm Ben. Daniel had to work. Hope that's not a problem. He wanted to come. Sorry," I babble.

"You should go and get some coffee or something," Anne instructs me as she leads Emma into her office. "We'll be an hour."

I head out into the bright light of day; the thought of having an hour to myself is tantalizing.

California dictates that until the birthmother signs the waiver, the adoptive parents are considered caretakers, not parents. Technically the birthmother has thirty days to sign the paperwork. That means on the morning of the twenty-ninth day Emma can wake up, change her mind and decide she wants to raise Zelda and that is that.

Or, after three days, she can waive the thirty-day waiting period and sign away her rights.

That is our hope.

Today, Anne will ask Emma what her intentions are vis-à-vis the waiver.

I should have brought something to keep my mind occupied. Instead, I wander the streets until my anxiety gets the better of me. With nowhere else to go my mind turns to Daniel.

He should have come this morning, I think. Couldn't he take one day off from his writing? Why does his work always come first?

Walking around the block for the third time, I start to question his desire even to have a baby. By my fifth go-around I am convinced that I have pushed him into something he didn't even want in the first place.

Mid-internal rant I catch myself. I have a tendency to create alternate paranoid realities. I find a bench and sit down. My initial response has been to lean on Daniel, to share my every fear with him, but I don't want to do that. I don't want to add to his anxiety or have him add to mine, so I stay silent.

It is time to exercise self-control. I am about to become a parent and ought to start acting like one.

Emma will sign the three-day waiver or she will not. This adoption will finalize or it will not. But either way this baby will be born. The three of us—Daniel, Emma and myself—have been brought together. Call it fate or chance but we have been given the responsibility—the charge—of ushering this life into the world, to guide this life into existence. That began the moment Emma chose us. Her decision linked the three of us and solidified an unspoken contract. An oath.

We are guides, I think.

Now I call Daniel. This is an idea I am excited to share.

Emma says nothing about the waiver when I pick her up and I don't ask.

"I'm really happy you are here."

She does not respond. And that is fine.

"Are you hungry?" I ask.

"I don't know."

Over the past several weeks I have begun to understand her language. No means no. Yes means maybe. I don't know means yes. She is hungry.

We go to California Pizza Kitchen, where she orders a Coke.

Not a Coke. Coke is terrible for the baby.

I distract myself with the menu while voices scream inside of my head.

Take care of my baby.

I sip my water.

You don't get a say. Not your baby. Not yet.

While we wait for our food I wonder if the couple at the next table assumes we are married. I wear a wedding ring and Emma is pregnant. She is not my wife yet she is the mother of my child.

After lunch, I drop Emma off at her apartment. As she steps out of the car she tells me she has been craving microwaveable frozen pretzels. I tell her I will bring some over tomorrow. It makes me happy to hear her ask for something.

Anne Brumer calls the house later that night.

"Emma has asked to sign the three-day waiver," she tells me.

"That's great," I say and give Daniel the thumbs up.

"She is definitely detached from the baby," Anne notes.

I nod, though I do wonder if this repeated observation is a cause for concern. "If I were placing my child I would detach as well," I repeat, hoping for confirmation. Daniel looks at me, puzzled.

There is the briefest pause.

"To be honest, it could go either way," she says without emotion. "Emma's detachment from the baby could be an indication of her clarity or it could signal that she is not fully conscious of what is going on and might, after the baby is born, change her mind."

"I'm going to choose to believe the former," I say, and thank her for her help.

Daniel agrees. We must accept Emma at her word. What other choice do we have?

"Either way we are her guides, right? Isn't that what you said?" Daniel asks. He smiles. "I thought that idea was great. Gives me a sense of peace."

"It's a nice word, guides," I say.

∽

"Fucking guides," I mumble. I am back at the window with the curtain balled up in my hand. Emma has left. The November night is dark and the cold seeps through the windowpanes. A car flies down our street. I follow the taillights until they disappear.

Wade into this nightmare, I think. Stop running from it.

Having a baby has revealed how little control we have in life.

You may not raise this child.

My breathing becomes agitated.

I want to guide her throughout her entire life.

I don't even try to stop the flow of tears.

You may not.

I cover my mouth. I don't want to wake Daniel. I know he would want to comfort me. I don't want to be comforted.

I drop onto the couch and pull myself into a tight ball. I lie in the dark and realize that I am no longer numb.

Be grateful for that.

Daniel wakes me up the next morning. I don't share my nighttime meltdown—that I am sleeping on the couch says plenty.

Later that afternoon I bundle Zelda up and take her out for a stroll. The sun is beginning to set. The previous night's meditation on fear has allowed me to let go a little, to accept the idea of being a guide, to embrace the beauty of helping to bring a life into the world.

When I approach the house there is not a single light on and I wonder if Daniel is still in his office writing. Zelda is asleep and I love the weight of her against my chest. For a brief moment I consider another stroll around the block, but something draws me home. As soon as I unlock the door I see what it is. Daniel is curled up on the corner of the couch in the living room in the dark. He has the blanket I slept with stuffed between his legs and holds it against his chest.

It is difficult not to think the worst but I wait for him to speak.

"Maybe..." he says and then stops himself. His gaze falls on Zelda's legs poking out from the Bjorn, but it is so dark I can't be sure. "Maybe," he shifts and draws the blanket into him. "Maybe we shouldn't fight this."

My hand presses into Zelda's back, and I am thankful for the physical connection to her, to her breath.

"Are we taking his child?" he asks. The pain in his voice is heartbreaking.

I close the door and collect myself. I recognize his fear but for a moment my anger surfaces.

I kept my darkness to myself. I don't want yours.

"Ben?"

I turn back around and take him in. He looks scared but I can't take care of him right now. I don't have anything left to give.

"Zelda is not his child," I snap.

"I just...." he stammers.

I flush with heat.

"Maybe we cut our losses. Maybe we save ourselves more pain. I can't lose her," he says. He swallows. "I was here and you were gone and I tried to imagine our life without her." He weeps. He is a full-body crier. "I felt sick, physically sick," he manages to get out. "I don't know how I would go on." He is inconsolable.

It is his turn to feel the possibility of true loss and profound love.

Dig deep; you do have more to give, I think.

I sit down on the couch, Zelda still attached to my chest. Daniel curls himself up even tighter. He does not want to be comforted. I know the feeling.

No need to do anything. Just be present.

His breathing slows and his crying subsides. Zelda shifts on my chest and Sadie stretches out across the living room floor. We stay like this for some time.

There is nothing to say. We both know that we will fight to the death before we give up our child.

FROM THE DEPOSITION OF LIAM FLYNN
JANUARY 2002

Q: Calling your attention now to the time that you learned Emma was pregnant. How did that come about?

A: She walked into the bar that we were at...

Q: And what did she say?

A: That she was pregnant...

Q: What did you say?

A: ...with my child, and that she was intending to take it to California and give it up for adoption.

Q: Did you tell her at the time that your ex-girlfriend had also told you that she might be pregnant?

A; Yes, she was pregnant.

Q: How did you find out it wasn't your child?

A: I never really did. I just didn't believe it was my child when it was born.

Q: But you believe that it might be your child?

A: No. I was unsure. It was not belief or disbelief.

Q: Just a maybe?

A: Just a possibility, yes.

ben barnz

17

It is Thanksgiving—hands down my favorite holiday. I love the food, the celebration of family and friends, and the complete absence of religion and gifting pressure. Daniel and Zelda are asleep beside me. I am awake just after 7 AM despite having done the 2 AM feeding. I require less and less sleep. There is much to do to get ready so the only thing keeping me in bed right now is my joy in listening to Zelda's steady breath; I can't get enough of it. It soothes me; for a few minutes I slow my breathing to match hers.

I get out of bed to begin cooking. This holiday pulls me east; I miss my New York City family and their traditions. I miss the constant picking as the turkey is carved, the overload of desserts, the loud exclamations over the beautifully set table, and my parents singing their college fight song with my aunt and uncle. I wonder what traditions we will build with Zelda.

Will this be our only Thanksgiving together?

I will not allow myself to fall down this rabbit hole, not today.

I check my email and am surprised to see an email from Scott Foster.

Email from Scott Foster, November 23, 2001:

In touch soon. Enjoy the holiday and more
importantly, your daughter. More soon.

Daniel leans against the back of my chair in order to read
Scott's email.

Another information-less email aggravates me. There is still
no information on a new judge. There is still no court date.

"I'm sick of his no-news casual bullshit," I snap and push past
Daniel who stands too close to me. I remove myself before I say
something I can't take back.

"Why aren't you fed up?" I say as Daniel walks into the kitchen.
"I mean does he even know what he's doing? Maybe we need to
find a new lawyer."

My anxiety runs close to the surface; anger spills out of me. I
begin to fall down the rabbit hole.

I don't want to lash out at Daniel, but he is here; there is no
one else.

He makes his way through the kitchen without stopping and
heads into the dining room, away from me, away from my anger.

Left alone, I take the turkey out of the refrigerator so it can
come to room temperature, then start on my mother's stuffing
recipe.

I hear Daniel beginning to set the table in the other room. I
can hear his frustration in the way he sets the table: in the way the
plates clatter, the way the silverware jangles. I can't tell whether
his frustration is with me or with Scott or with the entire situation.
We are so conscious of trying not to burden the other.

We are doing the best we can.

I hear the wooden pie hutch open and know Daniel is taking
out the wine glasses. We bought the hutch at a flea market. It
seemed so expensive at the time, but it's beautifully crafted and I
find myself grateful to own it.

Gratitude. There, I think.

I slice the onion and welcome the not-borne-of-any-emotion
tears. I sauté the onions with the minced liver; the thing that dis-
gusted me the most as a child has now become my favorite ingre-
dient.

Daniel lays out the napkins while I stir the onion mixture

with the breadcrumbs. We each have our jobs. I cook and he makes everything look beautiful. We often joke that of the two of us he is the "gayer" one, always straightening up after me. He has made me appreciate presentation more; the beauty of a well-set table, the mental clarity that comes with a neat house.

The house begins to smell delicious—and like year upon year of memory and tradition. I walk out to the garage to find the metal roasting pan, the one my mother gave me, the same as the one she uses to roast her turkey. It's stained and dented from years of use.

When I return to the kitchen, Daniel stands at the kitchen island holding several water glasses.

"I'm grateful for you," Daniel says. "Let's enjoy today." He leans in and gives me a kiss. "I'm grateful for Zelda too. Let's hold on to that as well."

"I'm grateful for you too," I say. "And I do love you."

"I know you do," he says and smiles. "I'm going to finish setting up."

Be grateful for him, I remind myself, and Zelda and Emma. And my family back east and all the friends who are about to descend upon us.

The turkey goes into the oven.

We take a break and read the newspaper. I press my ear against our bedroom door and hope Zelda is awake but all I hear is the low white noise of the sound machine.

A timer goes off: the turkey needs to be basted. After that, there is nothing to do but wait. Wait for the guests to arrive, wait for the turkey to be finished, wait for Zelda to wake up. Wait to get a date for our hearing in Minnesota, wait for a new judge. Wait to find out if we will have another Thanksgiving with Zelda.

"Your apple pies look so good," Daniel says.

Daniel and I have hosted this holiday every year since we started dating, but this year is different. This year we host as a family.

"Why thank you," I say. I hear Zelda babbling from the other room.

Zelda turns her head as soon as I open our bedroom door. Her ability to recognize us is new. How brilliantly you are designed, I think as I lift her up and into my arms. Just when I am spent and think I can't go another day, she doles out a new small miracle. Will I always be able to see the miracles? When you are ten, sixteen, thirty? Her babbling began two days ago. It surprised me because I had grown to love our shared silence. Now that I hear her finding her voice, I long to know what her voice will sound like.

I blow a raspberry onto her neck and she breaks into peals of laughter.

"The timer went off so I took the turkey out," Daniel says as he comes up beside me. "Is that right?"

"Yes, thank you," I say and then turn back to Zelda. "Let's get you dressed. But you have to leave," I tell Daniel and push him out of the room. "We want to surprise you."

I dress her in a thin-corduroy red dress with white tights and step out of the room. Suddenly I understand the mothers who frequent child beauty pageants.

"You look quite stunning," Daniel says to Zelda and takes her in his arms.

Her blond hair softly curls around her face.

The doorbell rings and friends begin to arrive, all eager to take turns holding Zelda. They ask her about her day and her red dress and whether she is excited for her first piece of apple pie. She moves from one set of arms to another and the outpouring of love toward her moves me as much as it unsettles me. When they hold her are they wondering if this will be our first and last year hosting as a family? I excuse myself to go to bathroom.

"Ben?" It's Daniel, followed by a gentle knock on the bathroom door. "Are you all right?"

I hear laughter coming from the kitchen.

"It's time to eat," he adds.

"I'm coming," I say as I step out of the bathroom. I squeeze his arm as I rejoin our friends.

I wonder what this holiday will be like for Emma, sitting around the table with her family. Do they also go around the table and say what they're grateful for? If so, what does she say this year?

18

The following Monday we receive an email from Scott Foster.

<u>Email from Scott Foster, November 29, 2001</u>:

We are set for 12/6 only if I do not get called
for jury duty.

At last, a date. In one week we will know something, and that
is better than the limbo we have been living in for the last four
months.

<u>Email to Scott Foster, November 29, 2001</u>:

Just got off the phone with Emma who is obviously very frustrated, upset, and scared that
her family will now find out. She said that the
lawyer he [Liam] chose works in the same
building where her grandmother used to be
a legal assistant. Spoke with Nicole earlier
who said to remind you that California WILL

appoint Liam a lawyer and one who is an "expert" in the field, if jurisdiction got moved to LA.

Thanks for everything and for getting the new court date.

It is difficult to trust a complete stranger with something this intimate and life altering. It tests us, our faith in the kindness of strangers, our faith in the law, our faith in human decency. Seeking comfort, we reach out to Nicole. She replies later that day.

Email from Nicole Morgan, November 30, 2001:

I spoke with Steve, and understand his strategy much better. He may call Emma as a witness, but will do so only if the other attorney calls his client. If he calls her as a witness, she will be cross-examined, and that won't help us. The fact that Emma would not stay in California doesn't help us.

Let's keep our fingers crossed. He is a good attorney, and is doing a good job. The bottom line is that there is a very good argument that the case should be heard in Minnesota, because the baby was conceived there, both birth parents are there, and the only reason the child was taken out of state is because Emma came here to place the baby for adoption. I think we have a good case in California. Minnesota is an unknown. I have to be honest with you.

Her last sentence bores into me, there is a metallic taste in my mouth. *I have to be honest with you.*

The night before the Minnesota court date, neither Daniel nor I sleep. My exhausted mind jumps back in time, seeking a happier time, a *once upon a time* before this nightmare began.

~

It is mid-August; the day is hot and humid. Emma is eight and a half months pregnant and we are at her sixth check up with Dr. Davis. Daniel and I flip through magazines. I fake cough to cover up the sound of the page I rip out of *Parenting Magazine*. There is a color I like for Zelda's room. Just as I fold it and stuff it into my pocket Dr. Davis appears. I pray he didn't see me.

"Hey," he says and smiles. "I was about to do an ultrasound and Emma thought you might like to see."

We have never been asked back during one of Emma's check-ups. We stand hesitantly, uncertain about what is about to happen.

"Follow me," he says and turns back down the hallway.

Daniel and I look at one another. I know the joy I see on his face is reflected on my own.

"Wait," I say and take hold of his arm. "Remember, we decided not to find out the sex of the baby."

"I remember," he says and we walk down the photo-lined hallway into an examination room. Emma lies on her back, covered by a loose fitting gown.

I want to hug her and thank her but I know better. We have grown closer in the last few weeks but our relationship is still somewhat formal. This moment is intimate, unexpected. There is no way she can comprehend what this gesture means to me.

In my most optimistic fantasies I never allowed myself to go so far as to imagine this moment.

"Thank you," I whisper to Emma.

She smiles and turns her head toward the monitor.

"If you can leave the gender vague..." Daniel says, as the image on the tiny monitor comes into focus.

Dr. Davis nods his head.

"There's an arm," Dr. Davis says, "and there," he pauses for the briefest moment, "is the heart."

Your heart.

No one speaks. I take hold of Emma's hand. I can't help myself.

Do you know we are waiting for you? Do you recognize our voices? Can you sense our excitement?

Dr. Davis breaks the silence.

"The baby looks great. I'll print you a copy."

A moment later he leads us out of the room while Emma gets dressed.

We return to the waiting area, again passing all the baby photos. This time I hold a photo in my hand, an image of our child.

Daniel and I sit and wait. He places his hand on my leg and with a look we know what must be done. Experiencing the sonogram changed everything, as did Emma's decision to allow us into the examination room. Not knowing was a way to protect ourselves, but it kept *us* detached as well.

"We would love to know the sex of the baby," I tell Emma once we are back in the car heading east on Wilshire Boulevard. "If that is still cool with you."

I glance into the rearview mirror and catch Emma's eye.

"Are you sure you want to know?" she teases.

"Yes," we say in unison.

"It's a girl," she says and a smile breaks across her face.

With three simple words, you arrive.

∾

December has arrived and the night's darkness seeps into the days, robbing us of sunlight.

Today is the day of the Minnesota trial.

Two thousand miles away Emma and Liam prepare to sit in a courtroom together. Emma will go alone, compounding my guilt. I wish her sister would go with her, but that is not up to me. Will Liam bring his sister?

Daniel and I go about our morning as if it were any other day. I toy with the idea of taking an Ativan but decide against it. I will feel everything today. I will not run away from it.

"Could the trial be over in one day?" I ask Daniel before he heads out to his office to bury himself in his work. That is his escape.

He does not answer my question.

"Hello?" I ask.

"I'm thinking," he says.

I am surprised this question hasn't occurred to either of us before.

"I have no idea," he says. "How do we not know this?" There is such sadness in his voice that it breaks my heart. "Do you think it might last more than a day?"

The question shakes me to my core. We were so focused on today as decision day, the thought that it might not makes me sick.

"Time will tell," he says, heading to his office.

There is no way I can sit around and wait so I strap Zelda into her Bjorn. Sadie leaps up as soon as she sees me head for the door but I leave her at home.

Zelda is big enough now to face out when she is in the Bjorn. She observes everything. I kiss her head constantly.

After walking for a while, I feel Zelda's restless energy. She needs to eat but I can't go back, not yet. I need to keep walking, keep moving. I am terrified.

Fantasies about staying away forever flood my mind. Could I get into my car with her and just drive away? I wonder if Daniel would understand.

Zelda begins to cry.

"Sshhh," I say and stroke her belly through the thick fabric of the Bjorn. "Sorry," I tell her. "Let's go get you some food. Neither of us is going anywhere," I say and force myself believe it.

When I open the door I am relieved that Daniel is nowhere in sight. If we had heard anything he would have been waiting by the front door. I unstrap Zelda from my sweaty chest and make her bottle as she rests on my hip.

She latches onto the bottle as soon as I sit down. She wraps her small hand around my pointer finger and stares up at me. If I could live in this moment forever, I would.

By the time she finishes the bottle she is sound asleep.

"Oh, thank god," Daniel says, as I step out of our room.

He is at the end of the hall and I look to see if he is holding a phone. But he isn't. No news.

"I can't concentrate," he tells me. "Will you sit outside with me?"

We sit down in the grass together, neither one of us saying anything. What is there to say? He begins to lay his head down in my lap when the phone rings. He is on his feet and inside the house in a second. I am unable to move. I don't think I have ever known such fear in all my life.

He steps out onto the patio with the phone up to his ear and races out to me.

"We won," he says.

I am so relieved that all I can do is stare up at him. "We won jurisdiction," he repeats.

All the sound drops out and I realize that I can't feel my feet. I see Daniel's mouth moving as he walks back and forth. Then I hear Daniel thanking Scott as if through some distorted sound machine before he stops in front of me. We look at one another—unsure, overwhelmed, elated. There is definite shock. I want Zelda in my arms but she is asleep. Daniel drops down next to me and we wrap our arms around one another.

<u>Email to Scott Foster, December 7, 2001</u>:

Words cannot express our gratitude. We spoke with Emma and she too was elated and relieved. It is so very odd to be so grateful to someone we have never met but we are. From the bottoms of all three of our hearts—thank you.

FROM THE DEPOSITION OF LIAM FLYNN
JANUARY 2002

Q: Since the baby was born, have you provided any support for her, for the baby?

A: The baby, no. No one has ever asked.

Q: Have you ever offered?

A: No.

Q: What have you done in terms of purchases to take care of the baby?

A: For supplies type of stuff? Cribs and whatnot?

Q: Correct.

A: I don't have to purchase any of that. I have plenty of friends with children, family with children. It's all going to be given to me.

Q: As we sit here today, do you have a crib set up for the baby?

A: No, not as we sit here.

Q: Have you purchased any baby clothes?

A: No.

Q: What kind of formula does the baby drink?

A: How would I know?

Q: So it is fair to say that you have not purchased any formula for the baby?

A: Fair.

Q: Have you purchased any diapers?

A: No.

Q: A car seat? Have you purchased a car seat?

A: I wouldn't have to purchase one.

Q: Do you have one in your possession?

A: No. I can get all this at a drop of a hat. It wouldn't take any effort at all.

Q: Are you aware of whether or not the baby has any medical problems?

A: No, I am not.

Q: Have you ever asked anybody?

A: No, I haven't.

Q: How old is the baby?

A: Four months.

Q: What does a four-month-old baby eat?

A: I don't know. Formula mostly.

19

In my attempt to answer the phone before it wakes Zelda I stub my toe on the corner of one of our suitcases. We are headed east for Christmas in a couple of days. It will be the first time our siblings and nephews and nieces will meet Zelda.

"Excellent news on winning jurisdiction," Jonathan says. I can hear the "but" coming. I run the other phone out to Daniel in his office, working away at his old wooden writing desk. The sunlight pours into the small room. Everything looks a little brighter today.

I fill Daniel in as I pass him the other phone.

"It's Jonathan, he was saying how great it was that we won jurisdiction."

"Yes, getting it moved here was critical," Jonathan continues. Here it comes.

"But..." he begins.

I knew there was a but.

"But it's not over."

We have no idea what Liam will do next. We hope he will stop, but if he doesn't, at least we fight on our home turf. That gives us a small sense of control, where we have felt absolutely none for months. I catch Daniel's eye as we try to assess each other's stress level: up and down, up and down.

"California laws are great at protecting adoptive parents," Jonathan presses on, "but they also allow the biological parents the right to contest. It is an uphill battle for them, but California does ensure they get a fair shot, that they get their day in court. And," he plows on, "so you know all the facts up front—if Liam does continue to contest the adoption, California pays for his lawyer, flies him here, puts him up, and even gives him a food stipend."

"So he has no incentive to stop," Daniel says.

"That may be the case." Jonathan's response is immediate and unemotional.

"That's infuriating," I snap and see Daniel smile; he likes it when I get riled up. "Liam does nothing for months and then gets a full ride?"

My blood boils.

"I understand this is frustrating," Jonathan says calmly, "but it is the law."

"So," Daniel jumps in, "he can choose to move forward, spend nothing *and* get an all-expense paid trip to California. Why wouldn't he keep going?"

"I'm so pissed," I say and head out into our yard. I need space around me.

"The thing you need to remember is that Nicole is a very good lawyer and the law is strong here. But I want you to know all the possibilities. This win was great for you guys and I wish I could tell you that it is over, but it's not."

Jonathan and Nicole made it clear from the get-go that California laws protect adoptive parents; that's why winning jurisdiction was so essential. But nothing is settled and the serenity we felt last night is gone.

A cloud covers the sun.

Intellectually, I understand everyone deserves their day in court, but I don't want to extend that right to Liam. That realization embarrasses me.

It's not as easy to hold on to your moral compass when it directly impacts you.

I think about my parents' response when I came out. How their liberal ideals were tested.

It is not always simple to embrace the right thing.

Liam has every right to move forward if he so chooses. I hope he doesn't but I can't stop him, nor should I.

"You need to explain all of this to Emma," Jonathan tells us.

I am happy to have an excuse to call Emma. I miss her. I wish I wasn't calling with potentially upsetting news, but I prefer she hear it from me.

"I know it's difficult but we just need to wait. There is a strong possibility that he will do nothing and it's nice that you get to head back home for the holidays with some good news. So enjoy your family," Jonathan concludes: "And let them enjoy your daughter. Because she *is* your daughter."

Until this is settled, there is no peace.

"Thanks Jonathan," Daniel says. "Happy holidays and thank you for everything."

It is now mid-day and I am suddenly very aware of my growling stomach. I forgot to eat anything for breakfast.

"I'll call Emma after I eat something," I tell Daniel as I head back inside.

I grab a wooden bowl and begin to make lunch. While I chop up an avocado and some cucumbers, I remind myself that we knew what we were getting into. We knew the risks that accompany adoption; we knew that until an adoption is finalized, it's not.

Daniel comes into the house just as I finish making us a salad.

"You start," I tell him and hand him a bowl. "I need to call Emma and get this over with."

Daniel says nothing as I step outside and dial Emma's number.

"I was just thinking about you," Emma says, and I know she means it. She sounds happy. She has a job waiting tables at a "better restaurant" and talks to me in very general terms about being home. She doesn't ask after Zelda so I just let her know she is thriving and leave it at that.

I am hesitant to get into it all—Liam's non-decision decision, our conversation with Jonathan, the uncertainty of it all. I know how quickly her joy will evaporate.

"Jonathan called this morning."

I hear her quick intake of air. How badly I want her to be able to put all this behind her, to move forward. "Jonathan wanted all of us to know that until Liam decides what he wants to do..."

It kills me to have to finish this sentence, but I do.

"...it's not over."

"I hate him," she says coldly.

"Me too," I let slip and instantly regret it. I should not engage with her on this level. When this is over I want Zelda to know Liam, if she chooses to, and I don't want any bad blood. But in this moment I do hate him. I hate him for what he is doing to Zelda, to Emma, to all of us.

Since I can't stop myself, I say, "I'm going to refer to him as The Devil from now on."

Emma falls silent and I fear I have overstepped myself.

"The Devil," she repeats, then laughs. "That's funny." Her voice drifts off as though she were contemplating an image of him with horns and pitchfork.

"Depending on what he does we may need you to come back to Los Angeles for the deposition."

"Just let me know when!" she exclaims, ready for a fight. "I *want* to tell my side of the story."

If this does continue, if she does come back to Los Angeles, I wonder if she will want to see Zelda.

"Are you taking Zelda back to New York for Christmas?" she asks, and I recall our first conversation when she told me she wanted to live in New York.

"Yes. First time back with her."

"Good luck with the flight," she says, and laughs again.

Two days later, we walk into the airport for our first flight as fathers, which thrills and terrifies me. Will we be the family on the plane that everyone resents? Five hours on a flight with a four-month-old baby is daunting. Zelda's carry-on bag is bulging with too much paraphernalia.

We make it through security. It is the first time we have flown since 9/11 and it feels different. With Zelda on my hip I lift our heavy diaper bag onto the conveyor belt, followed by our cumbersome car seat. I pass Zelda to Daniel so I can take off my shoes and belt, and then take her back while he does the same before unpacking our electronics and dop kits and liquids and and and...

"Maybe we'll consider *not* doing this every year," Daniel says, half-teasing; with both our families in one city, years of stressful holiday travel loom ahead.

Both our Jewish families oddly and heretically celebrate hardcore Christmases. Each year both families have a massive meal, piles of presents, cookies and milk for Santa, carrots for his reindeer; my family even established a Christmas Eve reading of 'Twas *the Night Before Christmas*. Both families are so committed to their separate traditions that only after lengthy deliberations did my family consent to move our celebration to Boxing Day, so Daniel and I could attend *both* Christmases *every* year.

At the airport gate, we listen for the now-meaningful announcement: "Parents with small children may now board." We jump up. Stumbling down the narrow aisle with our car seat and supplies, we are grateful for the head start. The flight attendants clock us. It is 2001 and two men and a baby is still a rare sighting. My defenses go up. Do they judge us? Do they think we don't know how to parent? But I am dead wrong. Within seconds, Zelda's infectious smile has won them over. Before we've even buckled in her car seat, one of the flight attendants asks to hold Zelda, who plays her role beautifully. As she smiles and coos, free drinks appear.

We feed Zelda a bottle to ease her ear pressure as we take off and she falls asleep. While she sleeps, Daniel and I read legal case histories of contested California adoptions. Nicole Morgan had sent these to us months earlier but we were too nervous to read them until jurisdiction had been resolved. Now we want to be better informed.

This is our crash course in California adoption law.

Nicole's cover letter reminds us about the writ of habeas corpus Liam will need to submit *if* he decides to move forward. Every day I am learning new legal terminology: the term habeas corpus literally means, "you have the body;" in our situation it means who will "have" Zelda's body. Who will care for her during the litigation process? If the court grants Liam's writ, Liam will take Zelda back to Minnesota immediately following the depositions to live with him until the trial, months later. Nicole explained that the likelihood of this happening was small, but "small" is *not* the same as not a chance in hell.

"That will never happen," Daniel says, as he sees me beginning to tense.

"You don't know that."

He looks at me but says nothing. I am right and we both know it.

Reading on, we learn that Liam is considered an "alleged or natural father, not a presumed father." In order for Liam to be granted the title of "presumed father," he would have to be married to Emma, or have lived with Zelda after her birth. As an "alleged father" the court can terminate his rights and "allow the adoption to proceed over his objection if it is in the child's best interest."

In 1992, the California Supreme Court held that a father can only try to stop an adoption if he has taken every reasonable step to "act like a parent" from the time he knew of the mother's pregnancy. Under these criteria, a biological father must do "<u>everything</u>" within his power and circumstances to assert his parental rights and to take responsibility for the child, and he must do so "<u>from the time he becomes aware of the pregnancy</u>."

"These seem good for us, right?" I ask, hating the neediness in my voice. Neither of us is a lawyer and the nuances of the legalities are complicated, to say the least.

"I think so," Daniel says, though I can hear the question mark in his voice. "But she only sent us the ones that support our case. So there must be cases out there that back him and his position, right?"

The flight attendant walks by and smiles. Disappointment crosses her face as she notices Zelda is asleep. I wonder what she would think if she knew what we were reading, what we were facing. Would she consider being a character witness? Would she sing our praises on the stand?

"You've got a good one there," she says. We thank her and turn back to the stack of reading sitting on our tray tables.

In 1993, the California Supreme Court took up a father's rights again. It held that the father is charged with the responsibility of keeping up with the mother of his child; it is not the woman's responsibility. If a man has sex with a woman of childbearing years, he must presume that she could have become pregnant and make sure he takes sufficient steps to act like a parent. If he doesn't, his rights can be terminated.

"This is fantastic," Daniel says. "It *is* insane to think it is just a woman's responsibility."

I am embarrassed that it never occurred to me to ask the women I had sex with if they had become pregnant. I certainly did not want to be a father at nineteen but what *if* one of them had become pregnant and I never knew?

By the time the plane touches down in New York, I'm feeling more confident. Still, I can't shake Jonathan's voice; *it's not over.* And Nicole made it all too clear that this case could go on for some time, that some cases have dragged on for years. Despite winning jurisdiction, the fight is far from over. What terrifies me now is the thought of raising Zelda until she is three or four years old only *then* to have her taken away.

As we make our way off the plane the flight attendant slips a bottle of wine into our diaper bag. "What a lucky little girl," she whispers conspiratorially.

The frigid air hits us like a sucker punch as we exit the airport. Wide red brushstrokes appear on Zelda's cheeks, revealing her Irish ancestry.

I see my mother in the passenger seat of her Toyota, bundled up in her winter coat, waving at us. She jumps out and takes Zelda in her arms. In the past, Daniel and I took a taxi; grandchildren open new doors.

"She's so big!" my mother exclaims, moving into the back so she can sit next to Zelda.

"How was your first flight as parents?" my father asks as he pulls away from the curb, but before I can answer I see a new email from Nicole on my Blackberry:

> Liam is moving forward. Deposition set for January 28, 2002.
> Please make arrangements to get Emma here.

Did we really think Liam would stop?

Daniel meets my gaze—he saw it too. Missing nothing, my mother registers our silent exchange. I smile and she leaves it alone.

Daniel emails me: we need to call Emma.

I write back: tomorrow.

We were hoping for a respite, a couple of weeks where we wouldn't have to think about the what-ifs.

Forty minutes later we pull up to my childhood home on the Upper West Side and unload the car. Little has changed in thirty-five years. 94th street remains a quiet, tree-lined block. A PEACE sign hangs in my parents' brownstone's vestibule; it has been there since 1967.

Undressing Zelda takes several minutes. I appreciate living in a warm climate without the need for constant dressing and undressing.

I carry Zelda over to the wall of family photos.

This is a photo of my mother when she was a little girl with her brother. "Do you like their fancy clothes?" I ask. "And these are my sisters, your aunts, Julie and Andrea," I murmur as I make my way down the hall. We stand atop a mountain in Switzerland during a summer family vacation. The three of us look so much alike with our 70s feathered hair blowing in the wind. I am twelve and my white painter pants are too tight. I show Zelda a picture of me from high school with ten friends dressed up for Halloween. I went as a groom, a friend is dressed as my bride. "I've never understood why this photo is on our family wall," I whisper. I am surprised at seeing a photo of Zelda hanging on the far end of the wall. She is in my arms and looks straight into the camera, her blond hair backlit by the sun. That my parents hung this photo on this wall speaks volumes; Zelda belongs here. She is one of us. She is family. I glance back down the hall and catch my father watching me. He blinks back tears and heads upstairs.

I move to the back of the house where I point out our backyard. "I had my Bar Mitzvah out there," I tell Zelda. "That's also where I buried my hamster, and learned to ride a bike." I peer down the flight of red stairs leading down to the pitch-black basement and laugh. "Going down there used to scare the shit out of me," I whisper.

When I go upstairs, my mother is already enjoying a glass of wine and Daniel is halfway through a bowl of thick pea soup she made for our arrival, a soup she makes every time we come to New York. I kiss her cheek.

I point out the oval dining table to Zelda and explain that it is not connected to the base and has fallen over more than once. Then I make my way into the living room. I show her my favorite napping couch of all time. Beside the couch is the spot where I took care of my baby cousin one Thanksgiving so many years ago. "I have been waiting for you all these years," I tell her.

My mother has walked into the living room and looks at me. What must it be like to watch your child become a parent?

The next day my sisters and their families come to meet Zelda. Julie's children, Caleb, eight, and Lena, five, sit on the couch and take turns holding Zelda. Andrea's daughter, Zoe, is ten months old and my mother takes a slew of photos of her two new granddaughters propped up against several pillows. Compared to the Ashkenazi coloring of the rest of my family, my daughter is startlingly blond and pale. My family's immediate acceptance of Zelda into the fold should not surprise me; even so I can't help but feel deeply moved. I am also struck by the fact that two men with a child does not faze this next generation in the least.

The following day we drive across town to spend Christmas Eve at Daniel's parents' apartment on East 52nd Street. His parents, siblings, nephews and nieces shower Zelda with more love. Both of his sisters have two children; everyone takes *more* photos, further solidifying Zelda's place as a member of our extended clan. I can't help but wonder if these will be the only photos of everyone with Zelda. Will these family photos be deleted or gather dust on some closet shelf? Will this be an uncomfortable chapter no one wants to talk about?

How deep do we really go with family?

I will always go as deep as you will allow me to go. Ask me anything.

I stop myself from pouring a third glass of wine and force myself to stay in the moment. One of Daniel's family's traditions is that each couple is responsible for one course, so the meal is long and decadent and always ends with his mother's traditional Buche de Noel.

In the morning, Santa appears for the first time in Zelda's life. We ooh and aah over gifts a four-month-old won't ever register or care about. After breakfast we hustle out the door in time for Zelda's nap and drive out to Southampton to do it all over again.

Knocked out by the morning's stimulation, Zelda is asleep before we pull onto the Long Island Expressway. Daniel and I welcome the silence; we speak only a handful of words during the two-hour drive to the beach.

As a town, Southampton manages to hold onto its small town feel despite the influx of so many uber-rich. My parents' decision to buy the house in the 1980s was not only a brilliant real-estate decision but a strategic way to make sure my sisters and I would always want to visit them. My mother once again figured out how to keep us all close. The house is a wood-shingled, three-story Victorian. Built in the 1890s, it has a large front porch and an attic with a round turret room, which I immediately claimed. A large, flat yard stretches behind the house. My sisters and I were all married here.

Daniel honks the car as we pull into the driveway and my parents run out to greet us. My father helps with our bags as my mother unstraps Zelda from her car seat and carries her into the house. The energy in the house is warm and frenetic; my sisters' kids run around, several pots bubble auspiciously on the stove and my brother-in-law, Alan, and his son, Caleb, play foosball. My mother loves this—the chaos overwhelms me; herein lies the profound difference between my mother and me.

I take Zelda back. "I need to change her," I tell my mother and make my way upstairs to our bedroom before anyone can stop me.

The attic is a large open space with two bedrooms. My room is a refuge, shaped like a hexagon with five large windows encircling the bed. During the day, sunlight streams in; at night the stars surround me. I lay down on the bed with Zelda and watch as she takes in the light bouncing around the room.

"Do you like this room?" I ask her as I hear footsteps come up the attic steps.

"How are you doing?" Daniel asks, pointedly.

"Good," I tell him with all honesty. "I'm happy to be here. But also happy to have this space."

"Agreed. And—" he adds with glee, "it's time for a drink."

We make our way back downstairs, and as we step into the kitchen everyone yells "Zelda!" Her eyes go wide. A silent beat, then a huge smile breaks across her face. My family applauds loudly.

As my sisters set the table, my mother pulls a turkey out of the oven, my nephew and niece fold napkins, and my father sits in the living room with a glass of scotch and his book—always a book—a world away; I whisper to Zelda, "This is your family."

"I'll help in a second," I say. "I just want to show Zelda the yard."

A light dusting of snow covers the ground and the fresh air feels good.

"This is where your Aba and Papa got married," I tell her and add, "*I* asked him."

∼

Shortly after we moved in together in the fall of 1996, I knew I wanted to spend my life with Daniel, but I have no idea what made me believe I could marry him. Not many spoke about gay marriage at the time. All I knew was that like my sisters, I too wanted to make a public declaration.

In 1997, we had been together two and a half years when we

planned a trip to Italy, where I secretly planned to propose. I designed rings and wrote a letter listing everything I wanted to do with him during our life together:

Number 30: *I want to marry you.*

I tucked the note and the rings into my jacket pocket every morning as we made our way through Florence and Tuscany. I waited with growing nervousness for the ideal location to reveal itself.

On more than one occasion, Daniel asked me if I was okay.

Two weeks into our trip, we found ourselves in the hill town of Siena. We wandered past the auburn-roofed homes that lined the cobblestone streets into the majestic main square. We had just enough time to take in the beauty of the fan-shaped plaza when large, dark clouds swept in, opened up and poured rain. Forced to find cover, we made a mad dash for the Duomo. Inside, we discovered the Piccolimini Library, a room housing ancient manuscripts with frescos depicting the life of a local Siennese man who eventually became Pope Pius II. The final fresco displays a gorgeous wedding.

I had found my location.

We made our way toward the back of the room and sat on two carved wooden seats; they looked like mini-thrones. The room was empty and silent. While Daniel took in the frescos, I reached into my jacket and placed my letter on his lap. He looked at me questioningly. I said nothing. He opened the letter and began to read. When he neared the end, I placed a tiny red box holding two rings on his lap. I wasn't sure I was still breathing. Daniel opened the box and stared at the rings held in place by two old-typewriter letters: D and B.

The two of us sat suspended in time.

Of course I assumed he would say yes. I had no back-up plan. It would be a long vacation if he said no.

"Well?" I pleaded.

"Yes. Sorry. Yes, of course," he finally replied. "Yes."

"Look inside the rings." I told him, flush with joy.

He read the words I had inscribed in each ring:

who we are

who we will be

"I need you to know something," he stammered a little, "I didn't respond right away because I never thought this would happen. I never thought this moment would happen in my life and I am so happy it did. And that it is you. I would love to marry you."

In that moment I understood something I did not before; that in this intimate, private moment, in the asking and the answering, the act was complete. We were married. The ceremony would be beautiful theater.

When we stepped out of the Duomo thirty minutes later, the dark clouds had disappeared, the sky was blue, and the bells of the cathedral began to ring out.

~

"Ben, come inside," Daniel says, as he pokes his head out the screen door. I turn to see my family inside; warm light and laughter spills out into the darkening Southampton yard.

"Coming," I say.

Before I go back inside I tell Zelda, "A year later, we had our commitment ceremony right there," and point out the large oak tree on the side of the house. "Even if it wasn't in *The New York Times*."

I had sent our announcement into *The Times* Style section— they had never announced a same-sex union in their pages. That was 1999. *The New York Times* wouldn't announce a commitment ceremony until September 2002, three years after our own, and one year after Zelda was born.

~

Hurricane Floyd ripped through the eastern seaboard two days before our September wedding. The tent was already set up and had to be lowered; tables and chairs folded up and put away. Daniel and I sat in front of the television watching The Weather Channel with increasing dread, convinced that no one would be able to fly in and that our wedding would take place in a muddy yard with only a few family members present. As in Siena, the weather blessed us: Floyd blew through with no damage and left a crystal clear weekend in its wake. Daniel wore a blood-red suit, I wore chocolate brown. We immediately wanted to establish a celebratory mood, so we served drinks as people arrived. Since so many of our friends knew each other, there was a familiar, joyous feeling from the beginning. Beneath the massive oak tree hung a patchwork quilt—our chuppah—that Daniel and I had sewed together. We chose warm and vibrant colors: vivid golds, deep reds and browns.

Every guest signed the katubah, since they were all there to bear witness. My aunt and uncle had just finished adding their names when the screams of my niece Lena pierced the air. Her father had been spinning her in the air, not realizing she was holding Daniel's ring, which had just flown out of her tiny four-year-old hand. A friend organized the guests into a line to scour the lawn but the ring was never found.

An hour after drinks began, a friend of Daniel's stood with us beneath our chuppah and began to sing Puccini's *O Mio Babbino Caro*. Daniel and I had no interest in walking down an aisle. We loved that the song would act as an invitation to begin. The guests quieted as her voice carried across the lawn and by the middle of the song everyone was seated. For the ceremony, friends and family members chose readings. At the end, Daniel and I exchanged vows and our nephews and nieces took our hands and helped us smash the glass.

Then the party began.

Bottles of wine dotted the long tables lit by hundreds of tea lights. Colored lanterns reflected in the clear top tent. Then our five-course Tuscan feast began. For years we would be mocked because of the number of toasts.

Beautiful theater indeed.

~

When I wake up in my attic room two years later, I see Zelda happily gurgling to herself in her pack 'n play. I wonder how long she has been awake.

"Happy Boxing Day," I say, leaning over and smiling down at her. "I hope you marry a British guy so we can keep this tradition alive."

"Or woman," Daniel laughs.

"Should we see if British Santa came?" I ask Zelda, lifting her into my arms.

We make our way downstairs where Caleb and Lena are already in the kitchen. They have been awake for hours; my sister and her husband are on their third cup of coffee.

"Finally!"

The kids drag us over to the porch door so they can show Zelda the chewed-up carrots devoured by the reindeer. We head into the living room for further proof: half-eaten cookies and an empty glass of milk. Santa even left a note, though no one can explain why he appears illiterate and has atrocious penmanship.

Zelda has her first experience with my mother's excessive giving. There are piles and piles of presents stacked in front of the fireplace.

We spend a few more days at the beach where the freezing weather keeps us inside. I rarely let Zelda out of my sight. The uncertainty of our future makes me selfish.

It isn't until we are back on the plane that I begin to understand how significant this trip east has been. Zelda has shifted a paradigm, not just for Daniel and me, but also within our families. We are no longer the youngest sons and youngest brothers. We are fathers.

When we land back in Los Angeles, I immediately feel the weight of our impending litigation.

"How are you doing?" Daniel asks, as he pulls onto the Freeway. The breeze blows through the car and it looks as though Zelda is trying to catch the wind with hands.

"Fine," I say—and almost believe it.

At the house, Zelda arches her back as I unstrap her from her seat.

"What's going on?" I laugh.

She reaches for the door before I am able to get out my keys.

"Stop," I demand. "You're going to fall out of my arms."

Sadie leaps up as soon as I open the door and runs around our feet, her tail waggling wildly. Zelda giggles with delight. She leans down in an attempt to pet her dog.

Zelda recognizes her home.

We leave our bags by the door so we can attack the piled-up mail. *The New Yorker*, *Food & Wine*, holiday cards. At the bottom of the pile is a letter we almost miss.

It is from a woman named Janet Chan, and she is Zelda's court-appointed lawyer.

I hear Jonathan's voice in my head: it is not over.

"Look at you," I say, trying to ignore the blood pounding in my head, "with your own lawyer."

Daniel looks at me with a crooked smile.

The letter informs us that Janet needs to meet her client.

20

In an effort to shake up our walking routine, I drive Zelda to the Hollywood Reservoir with its sweeping views of Los Angeles.

It's 10:30AM and there are only a few cars in the parking lot. Zelda is super alert, her head craning to follow a bicyclist as he whips by. The sun's reflection on the water grabs her attention next, as does a small barking dog. "Please don't like small yappy dogs when you grow up," I say. When I am halfway around the reservoir my phone rings.

"Janet Chan is coming in an hour." Daniel's voice is pitched high and tight

"To our house?" I ask realizing immediately the idiocy of the question. "What the fuck?" I add, and then smile apologetically at Zelda, as if she cared.

"I don't know. Perhaps it's some kind of surprise attack thing to see how we really live. Either way you need to come home now."

"Of course," I say turning back toward my car. "Thank god for my high school race-walking class."

Daniel will have the entire house straightened in minutes, but even so I am a half hour from our house, so I pick up my pace.

I call Daniel from the car.

"I'll do the dishes when I get home," I say.

"Already done."

Today everything must be right. Even I, as sloppy as I am, understand this. Today Zelda's lawyer will meet her new client. Today is our first opportunity to prove ourselves as Zelda's parents.

When I get home everything is neat and spotless. An outfit is laid out for Zelda and her blanket is draped over her co-sleeper. Daniel is in the den, opening the French doors.

"The house looks great," I tell him, passing Zelda off before I hurry into the bathroom to clean myself up.

"Should we dress her business casual?" I joke from the bathroom.

"I was thinking more cocktail party. It is her first meet-and-greet."

Zelda turns her head toward me as I make my way into the hallway.

"I think she liked the cocktail party idea," I say and lift her from Daniel's arms. Her soft blond curls fall across her forehead and she smiles. The smell of baby as intoxicating as ever.

I kneel next to Sadie, who licks Zelda's hand, which prompts Zelda to giggle.

"We have to get a move on, missy. You've got a lawyer to meet."

I take her into our room and put her in a pink floral dress with a muted flower design and a pair of matching bloomers. Daniel chose well.

There is not much to do once we are all dressed but wait for Zelda's lawyer to arrive. Daniel feeds Zelda her bottle in the den. The sight of my husband feeding our child never ceases to astound me.

The doorbell rings. I make my way to the door and past the kitchen where I notice that Daniel has laid out a tray with a pitcher of water and some cheese and crackers.

"You're good," I say over my shoulder.

"Showtime," I hear him say.

A short, harried woman introduces herself as Janet Chan. I see her eyes scan the living room as she enters.

"I'm Ben," I say and put my hand out a little aggressively. "This is Daniel," I add, as he joins us. Zelda is on his hip with a bottle in her mouth. "And this is Zelda." Even I can hear the grating perkiness in my voice.

"It's nice to meet you," she says, then turns to Zelda. "Especially you." She speaks in a baby-ish tone and I immediately judge her for it. I think I see Zelda furrow her brow.

Janet drops her oversized black bag next to the couch as Daniel offers her some water.

I search Janet's face to try to get some kind of read on her attitude toward us—that she thinks we are great parents, that she is on our side.

"Would you like to see the house?" Daniel asks.

She asks a lot of questions about the Co-sleeper, and reveals that she has a daughter exactly Zelda's age. Daniel and I exchange a quick look, both wondering the same thing: will her baby affect her judgment? And if so, how?

While I follow her down the hallway I argue both sides to myself. On the one hand, that she has a child Zelda's age might be good for us. She will sympathize with our attachment. She knows firsthand all that goes into caring for a child. On the other hand, she could feel that nothing trumps the biological bond.

By the time we enter the den, I can feel the sweat on my forehead. We point out all the books we have for Zelda, noting her "favorites." I see Daniel left a few books on the floor beside the rocker, suggesting we were mid-read when she arrived.

I wink at Daniel, and then tell Janet that this room will eventually become Zelda's bedroom.

Because she is still going to be with us, right?

Janet nods briskly and Daniel leads our small group out into the yard. She admires our fruit trees and mentions that she covets an office like Daniel's. I can see the house through her eyes, it feels warm and inviting. We make our way back through the kitchen and into the living room just as Zelda finishes her bottle.

"Your home is lovely," Janet says and helps herself to some cheese.

She asks a slew of questions about Zelda. She asks about her sleeping and eating habits, which are easy to answer. She asks us if there are activities Zelda especially likes.

She is four months old, are you kidding?

"She loves when we read to her," I reply quickly. "And she loves going on long walks around the neighborhood."

She sounds like a perfect date.

"And she loves her dog," Daniel adds. Semantics is everything: "her" dog makes Zelda a part of our family. *Not* Liam's.

"Well," Janet says, slipping her oversized purse onto her shoulder, "it was nice meeting you. Zelda seems well and you both seem very good with her." She stops at the door and adds, "Liam arrives next week for the depositions." She adds, somewhat ambiguously. "We'll see how that goes."

And then she is gone.

We remain silent as we watch her walk down our front path, the three of us framed in our doorway, a different kind of Norman Rockwell painting.

"Do you think it matters that she has a kid the same age as Zelda?" Daniel asks through his teeth as he waves a final goodbye.

"I have no idea," I say and head back into the house. "Why? Fuck. I hate this."

"Could be good for us, right?" he asks. "I mean, wouldn't she relate to having a baby in the house?"

I nod, happy to latch on to his reasoning. "But it could work the other way as well. She could think that biological connection is everything."

We go back inside and close the door.

"Well, either way, you did very well," I tell Zelda, "and now it is time for a nap."

21

Janet Chan calls mid-January to arrange a visit for Liam with Zelda when he comes for the depositions.

"We'll meet at the Denny's in Santa Monica on Sunday," Janet says.

I find myself angry that Liam will meet Zelda before Emma, and I struggle to keep the irritation out of my voice as we make the arrangements. I remind myself that I need Janet on our side.

She tells me Liam is staying close to the airport and won't have a car. I wonder if I detect a hint of pity in her voice. While she talks, all I can think about is what a ridiculous idea it is to meet at a Denny's. How can someone with a four-month-old baby think that a crowded diner will make for a good visit with a baby? I decide she either wants the meeting to go poorly or she is an idiot.

I sit outside our front door waiting for Daniel, chomping at the bit to share the news with him. When I see him turn the corner with Zelda and Sadie I run to join him.

"Denny's?" He is incredulous.

"Right? Fuck her. Fuck him. I don't want to do it," I say, hardly giving him a moment to absorb the news.

"And it's on Sunday! The same day Emma arrives."

I can feel my aggression building and do nothing to stop it. I reach out to unstrap Zelda from her Bjorn.

"Stop," Daniel says and gently pushes my hand away. "What's going on with you?"

The question only annoys me more. "Let's say no," I say, not even looking at Daniel. "Let's tell them we don't want to do it."

"It's a good idea," Daniel says calmly, which infuriates me even more.

Just agree with me, I think.

Of the two of us, Daniel tends to be the more rational. "Us going will show everyone that we're open and not afraid of him," he continues. "Plus it will show Liam how happy Zelda is."

"We're supposed to meet them at a *Denny's*," I scoff, not quite ready to agree with his sensible thinking.

"That *is* a stupid idea. I'll give you that."

"Well, I don't like it," I say petulantly, knowing he is right. "But fine."

~

The following Sunday we wake up to the sound of pounding rain.

Daniel and I spend the morning playing with Zelda and reading the newspaper; neither of us wants to be alone.

Janet Chan never explained how the visit would work. So while Zelda takes a brief morning nap, I pack some toys, a few diapers, a change of clothes and a bottle. Zelda has been phasing out her morning nap so I am happy that after only half an hour she wakes up and can distract me.

Around 11:30, Daniel and I make a snack. We both pick at our plates, unable to eat.

"I'm going to skip her afternoon nap," I tell Daniel.

He looks at me for a moment as he realizes my plan—to make Zelda sleep deprived and irritable.

"I won't make this easier for him," I say getting up from the table and heading into the kitchen. I don't want to hear Daniel tell me I'm being petty and unfair. I carry Zelda into the other room to read her a book.

At one, we drive west to Santa Monica. The rain continues,

and it brings me an ugly joy that Liam is not experiencing sunny California weather. I turn the radio up in the car to prevent Zelda from falling asleep.

When we arrive at Denny's, I tuck Zelda under my coat and run inside to the crowded and loud diner. We find Janet inside, pacing. She has a tight, nervous energy but this might just be her nature. She smiles and I choose to read it as a sign that she is on our side, that she understands how awful this must be for us.

"Liam's already here with his lawyer," she says, and gestures toward one of the round booths in the middle of Denny's where a young man sits in a baseball hat with a middle-aged, heavy-set man. Janet does not suggest that we meet Liam, and suddenly her attitude baffles me. Is she with us or against us?

Liam's hat is pulled down low over his face; I can't see what he looks like. The image only underscores his role as The Dark One. He places a plastic airport bag next to the condiments in the middle of the table and pulls out what looks like a small white stuffed animal with a pink bow. Everything feels bleak: the restaurant itself, the damp, dreary weather, the noise, Zelda rubbing her eyes.

I wonder if Janet regrets her choice of locations.

Janet continues to make no sign that she will introduce us to Liam or his lawyer, so we are left standing by the Denny's cash register, uncertain how to proceed. Zelda drops her head onto my shoulder, and I feel regret and shame for not allowing her a nap. I take off her coat.

"Why don't you two grab a table?" Janet finally suggests.

There is a small booth close to where we stand with a partition that will allow us to keep an eye on Zelda. I sit with Zelda. She squirms. Janet hovers, anxiously looking back and forth between Liam and us.

My instincts tell me not to trust her.

Daniel takes control. "How's this going to work?" he asks. "You're taking Zelda over to him and they're just going to hang out at the table?" I can hear the subtle disdain in his tone and I wonder if Janet picks up on it.

"That's the idea," she says, reaching for Zelda. I have to stop myself from smacking her hands away.

"I love you," I whisper into Zelda's ear so she can carry my voice with her, just as Janet reaches down and lifts her from my arms.

"Let's see how it goes," I hear her say with her back to me.

I watch this fucking stranger maneuver her way through the

busy restaurant with my daughter in her arms. I fantasize about tackling her, grabbing Zelda and running. I know Janet is only doing her job, but I hate her. Suddenly, I understand the stories of parents miraculously lifting cars off their children.

Daniel reaches across the table and takes hold of my hand.

"You're doing great, babe," he says.

I pick up a menu and pretend to read.

Daniel asks me if I want something to eat.

"Yeah, right."

He looks at me.

"Sorry," I say. "Sorry."

I glance over at Liam's table. For a moment I can't see Zelda and my heart stops.

A waitress approaches our table and asks us if she can get us something to drink.

"Two black teas, please. With milk," Daniel says.

Janet sits down at the table. I focus on my breathing.

I force myself to watch Liam as he tentatively takes Zelda in his hands. I long to see his face, to hear his voice but he is too far way and his cap is too low.

What must that be like for him, I think and then hate myself for even wondering. I am torn between anger and curiosity: what must it be like for Liam to hold his biological child?

He is the enemy, I remind myself.

Liam leaves his baseball hat on and I wonder if Zelda can even see his eyes. He awkwardly balances her on the edge of the table, then looks at Janet with an expression that seems to say: *now what?* No matter how hard I strain to hear, I can't make out Liam's voice through the noise of the restaurant.

The waitress delivers our tea. Daniel tells her we are not going to order food but we promise to leave a big tip.

Out of the corner of my eye, I see Liam speaking to Janet and his lawyer. They respond but do nothing to help with Zelda.

"Strange how disinterested Janet seems, right?" Daniel asks, as though he read my mind. My mouth is dry and all I can do is nod.

Is it really possible that she has a baby the same age? How can she stop herself from reaching for Zelda?

I hope Janet's detachment means that she will stay neutral. She leans over the table and I glimpse Liam grabbing the stuffed animal. He moves it in front of Zelda's face. When she doesn't respond he moves it closer, which causes Zelda to arch away from him. Then I hear her begin to cry and all the restaurant noise drops away. I sit on my hands. A moment later, Janet walks toward our table with Zelda.

"She's fussy," she offers flatly. "Seems she misses the two of you."

I glance at Daniel. Does that mean something?

I take Zelda in my arms and stroke her back. I whisper in her ear: "Hey angel, I'm right here." Everything is going to be okay.

"Give me a minute with her," I tell Janet with a smile. We need this woman on our side. Zelda begins to calm and I make sure Janet sees.

I take Zelda to a small hallway leading to the bathrooms where it is quieter. A large mirror hangs on the wall. I play a game with Zelda where I lurch her toward the mirror and then back, causing her to giggle. When I turn back to the dining room I realize Daniel and Janet have been watching. Neither says a word but Daniel smiles at me. Guilt gets the better of me: I know Zelda is partially fussy because I didn't let her have her nap. Hoping to correct a wrong I hand Zelda back to Janet while she is still happy.

"We'll try one more time." Janet brings Zelda back to Liam.

"We'll get through this," Daniel says as we sit back down. "But nice work with the mirror game."

"This is hard," I mutter.

"The worst."

I take hold of his hand.

"It will be okay," I say.

Please let that be true.

A moment later Janet returns. Zelda is crying.

"All right. The visit is over," she says.

There is something in her tone that feels accusatory, as though she blames us. For a paranoid minute, I wonder if she figured out that I skipped her nap, but it is over, that's all that matters. The visit is over.

"We'll see you tomorrow for the depositions," I say, while Daniel leaves cash on the table. Neither of us touched our tea. We exit into the pouring rain without a glance back. Zelda falls asleep almost as soon as I put her in the car seat. The phrase "dick move" repeats over and over in my head. Then I think about Jonathan's "I like to win" comment. I take off my glasses and rub my eyes. Daniel is silent; the only sound, the steady rain and the rhythmic swish of the wipers.

At home I head into the bathroom and repeatedly splash water on my face, wrestling with the image of Liam holding his biological child. What is Zelda's connection to this man?

Daniel reminds me that Emma flies in today and that her plane is on time. It is not like me to forget something like this and I find it unsettling.

The state of California does not pay for Emma to be included in these proceedings, so it falls on us to bring her here.

"I'm excited to see her," I say, determined to leave Denny's behind.

After an early dinner I am back in the car. The rain has stopped and the clouds have disappeared. As I approach the airport, I wonder which hotel Liam is staying in.

So much has changed since we picked up Emma the first time. Six months ago 9/11 hadn't happened. Six months ago I had no child. Six months ago my child had no lawyer.

Since I am no longer able to meet her at the gate, I wait at baggage claim. I am taken aback as I watch her walk toward me, a smile spread across her face. Her pregnancy weight is gone. There is a lightness about her that was absent before.

"Hi," she says, wrapping her arms around me.

"Hi."

Her former guardedness has also disappeared and she radiates a naturalness and ease that makes me love her even more.

"How are you doing?" I ask as we head to the car.

"I'm good. Glad to be in warm weather and ready to kick The Devil's ass." Her laughter is warm and pure. I've missed her clarity.

We are a team now, bound by our will to fight and our shared anger.

I drive Emma to a hotel in West Hollywood called Le Reve. A month earlier I had booked a room in the same hotel, and stole Daniel away for a three-hour tryst.

I am relieved to discover that a different person works the front desk. The other clerk was utterly bewildered when we checked out after only a few hours.

As Emma and I make our way down the hallway, I realize they have put her in the same room; there is a cosmic humor that Zelda's birthmother should share a bed with Daniel and me.

"Are you okay if I just go to bed?" she asks as we enter the room. "I worked this morning and am exhausted."

"Of course," I tell her. "We have to pick you up early anyway. We'll come get you at nine."

Before I close the door I ask if she is nervous about tomorrow.

"Not really," she replies without hesitation. "I'm just going to tell the truth."

22

January is almost over. The depositions are in the morning and I can't sleep. Images from yesterday's Denny's debacle play themselves out in my mind: the depressing interior, Liam shoving the stuffed animal in Zelda's face, the annoyed waitress, Janet's tight smile and Zelda, sweet Zelda, exhausted and in tears.

Daniel flips on to his side, he is having a restless night's sleep as well.

The clock reads 1:30 AM. Zelda will need to eat in a half hour.

"Fuck it," I whisper and sneak out of the room.

I turn off the house alarm and step into the yard in my T-shirt and boxer shorts. It feels good to be outside despite the January chill. The moon is nowhere to be seen but its brightness fills the yard with a cold, blue light. When my feet start to tingle, I head back inside to warm Zelda's bottle. Trying not to disturb Daniel, I steal back into our room and make it to Zelda just before she wakes up. I experience such joy from our synchronicity.

I lift her small body onto my shoulder, and walk into the den where I settle down on the rocker. The middle of the night feeding has become a kind of meditation for me. Zelda drinks voraciously, half-awake, half-asleep.

What will your first word be? I think.

Then: Please be around so I can hear your voice.

Zelda wakes up briefly after finishing her bottle and for a moment we lock eyes.

"What's it like to have no words?" I ask as her eyes flutter shut and her head becomes heavy as she gives in to sleep.

I can feel her exhaustion but I don't want to go to sleep. I don't want tomorrow to come. I don't want to sit and listen to Liam's side of the story. I don't want to humanize him. I don't want to find out that he has a story to tell.

Fatigue overtakes me as I walk down the hallway and back into our room. I slip into bed and am asleep as soon as my head hits the pillow.

When the white noise of our sound machine gives way to the church bells of our alarm I feel a sense of peace and calm. I remember Emma's words: *I'm just going to tell the truth.* Almost immediately I wonder—does truth always prevail?

Stop.

In the bathroom mirror I can see the toll that this constant push and pull has taken on me. There are bags under my eyes and creases on my forehead that didn't exist a few months ago.

"I told Emma we would pick her up at nine," I tell Daniel when I join him in the kitchen. "I wonder if she'll ask to see Zelda."

"You think?" he asks. "She hasn't asked before." He hands off Zelda. "I'll be ready in five minutes," he says and starts out of the room.

"Ana should be here any minute," I say as the front door opens. Ana recently started babysitting for Zelda; she is from Nicaragua. She is lovely and kind and generous with her extensive child-rearing knowledge. And Zelda loves her. After three months I am grateful for the help.

"I think someone is excited to see you," I tell Ana as Zelda reaches for her. "I just fed her a bottle so she's good."

"I'll take her to the park," Ana says and then repeats it to Zelda, "Should we go to the playground? Go on a swing?" Zelda reaches up and gently touches her face.

"We should be home sometime this afternoon," I tell Ana and kiss Zelda quickly. If I linger I may lose it.

"Should we have spoken to Ana about the trial?" I ask Daniel as we pull out of the driveway.

"I don't think so, no," Daniel responds and turns on the radio. The distraction is a relief for both of us.

As we pull up to the hotel Daniel says, "Wow, she looks great." Emma is waiting outside.

He throws open his door and leaps out to give Emma a long hug. She is in a light blue tailored blouse and dark skirt; her hair is down and more blonde than I remember it.

"Good morning," I say. "How'd you sleep?"

"Great!" she exclaims. "So ready for this," she adds and climbs into the back seat.

We talk about her cats and her sister and what it's like to be home. She tells us about the restaurant where she works. "Nicer than the restaurant I worked in before I came to L.A." We take our cue from her and talk about everything around Zelda without talking about Zelda herself.

Since the traffic is light, we arrive earlier than expected at The Edelman Children's Court of California in Monterey Park. The courthouse is imposing, architecturally bland and sterile. We walk through the lobby at nine-forty; the first to arrive for the depositions at ten. I peek into our conference room just off the main lobby and see a lone stenographer sitting in front of her stenotype.

"Hello," I say.

"Hello," she replies, flatly.

Daniel suggests we wait outside.

"It's been freezing back home," Emma says, and leans against a low concrete wall. "It's so nice to be somewhere warm."

Five minutes later, Liam, his lawyer, Janet and Nicole all walk out of the parking structure together. I find myself wondering what awkward conversations and introductions occurred in the parking structure's elevator.

Emma and Liam don't acknowledge one another; the rest of us exchange curt hellos. Now that I am able to get a good look at Liam I find myself perversely pleased with how good-looking he is. Over six feet, he has fantastically thick eyebrows and a strong, square jaw. He appears removed, a feeling heightened by his dark aviator sunglasses. Emma downplayed his looks, though I suspect her anger clouded her opinion. As I glance between them I think superficial thoughts about what the biological daughter of two such beautiful people will look like.

Zelda definitely has his eyebrows.

Daniel catches me staring at Liam and I can tell that he is

thinking the same thing.

We all walk back into the lobby and enter the conference room where the stenographer waits. The windowless room feels like an underground elementary classroom: long tracks of fluorescent lights hang overhead and give off an audible hum; a heavily used whiteboard runs the length of one wall; with partially erased notes.

I nod at the stenographer who remains emotionless; she is meant to be invisible. What must it be like to silently record the intimate details of other people's lives?

"How are you doing this morning?" Nicole asks Emma, and gestures for her to sit on one side of the stenographer. Nicole takes a seat next to Emma and motions us further down the table. Liam sits across from Emma with his lawyer next to him; Janet positions herself next to Liam. This surprises me.

Nicole introduces us to Liam's lawyer. He is a white, middle-aged man with a paunch. He and Nicole make small talk as they take out their paperwork, and Liam and Emma exchange a brief nod. Liam still wears his sunglasses and makes no move to take them off.

I lean forward and smile at Emma, wishing I could be next to her for moral support. She returns the smile. She is in total control. Daniel takes a yellow legal pad out of his briefcase. For a moment I wonder if it is the same pad I used to take notes when I spoke with Emma for the first time.

Emma turns her gaze to Liam and coolly stares at him. The tension between them is palpable. Still I admire Emma's fortitude and hope Zelda will inherit it.

Nicole passes us a note telling us that the judge will have a decision on Liam's Habeus corpus request by the end of the day. Is it really possible Liam could fly back to Minnesota with Zelda tomorrow? We look at her with obvious concern in our eyes but she shakes her head gently. She is unconcerned, but there is a chance she is wrong—and that chance terrifies me.

The depositions begin at 10:02 AM. Liam slouches in his chair, legs wide. He never removes his sunglasses.

FROM THE DEPOSITION OF LIAM FLYNN
JANUARY 2002

Q: Please state your full name for the record.

A: Liam, L-I-A-M, Flynn, F-L-Y-N-N.

Q: You are 25?

A: Correct.

Q: You are employed?

A: I work in a warehouse. It's...do all kinds of jobs. I basically mostly count, do inventory work.

Q: How long have you worked there?

A: Four, almost four months, yeah.

Q: How much money do you earn?

A: $8.75 an hour.

Q: How many hours a week do you work?

A: 40 plus.

Q: What is your career goal? What do you want to do?

Liam's lawyer objects over relevance.

Q: What are your plans?

A: Do I have to answer?

His lawyer nods yes.

A: I would like to do something creative. That's all I can really say for sure. Possibly graphic arts. Something like that.

Q: Have you ever been convicted of any crimes?

A: No.

Q: Including driving under the influence?

A: Is that a crime?

Q: Have you ever used illegal drugs?

A: Yes.

Q: What drugs?

A: Marijuana.

Q: Anything else?

A: No.

Nicole consults her notes. The questions continue. Liam answers without emotion. An hour passes.

Q: During the couple of months that you went
   out [with Emma], how was your relationship?

A: Had a lot of fun.

Q: Would you characterize it—go back to that
   point in time—would you characterize it as a
   serious relationship or a casual relationship
   or—

A: Pretty casual.

Q: You and her weren't making long-term plans,
   that's fair to say?

A: Not at that point, no.

Q; Did you and she have a sexual relationship?
A: Yes, we did.

Q: And who broke up with whom?

A: It was neither one of us. Really, we just both
   kind of went our separate ways.

Q: About how long went by before you saw her?

A: At least a month.

Q: And then what happened?

A: I saw her out. We talked briefly. She said she

wanted to talk to me, and I waited for a little bit, and she was busy so I left and called her the next day.

Q: You saw her at her place of work?

A: No.

Q: You said she was busy. She was talking to somebody else? So you called her the next day. What do you remember of that conversation?

A: I didn't actually speak with her. I called probably three times and never got an answer or call back so I just left it that.

Q: So did you ever speak with her in March other than—

A: No.

Q: Then when is the next time you spoke with her?

A: June 17th. That's when she informed me she was pregnant.

I find myself watching the stenographer, wondering about her silent role and the stories she has been privy to in this room. Another hour passes.

Q: During the September 12th conversation, did you ask him [Mr. Ross] any questions about where the child was placed?

A: No.

Q: Did you ask him how the child was doing?

A: No.

Q: Did you ask him any questions about the sex of the child?

A: Yes.

Q: And did he tell you?

A: Yes, he did.

Nicole finishes her questions; it is twelve-thirty. Two and half hours have flown by.

"I think we all need a break," Nicole says and packs up her briefcase.

"Couldn't agree more," Liam's lawyer responds and laughs. "Let's all lunch and start again in forty-five minutes."

"I have some calls to make," Nicole says to us.

"Wait," I blurt out and reach across Daniel to stop her. Daniel looks surprised, but I need some sort of reassurance. "What do you think?" I whisper.

"This is a marathon, not a race, and it's not over until it's over."

She can see the concern in my eyes, because she adds, "I got what I needed, so that's good. Now I really have to use this time." And she is gone.

We are all drained. The cafeteria is in the basement of the courthouse; like high school, we all break into cliques. Liam sits with his lawyer. I am relieved that Janet does not join them. Toward the end of our break, Liam's lawyer approaches our table and apologizes for Liam's sunglasses. He explains that Liam forgot his real glasses at the hotel and can't see without a prescription.

7. There are always two sides to every story.

Emma, Daniel and I decide to walk outside for some fresh air before Emma's deposition. As we walk outside I think about how much our relationship has changed. At first, we were business partners, negotiating a mutually agreed-upon transaction. When Liam chose to contest the adoption, he inadvertently helped us to create a richer, closer relationship with Emma. Had he stuck with his original impulse, that adoption was the right thing to do, we would not have become as close to Emma as we are now.

As if she can read my mind, Emma looks up at me, and smiles.

I excuse myself to check on Zelda.

When we reenter the deposition room, Janet is standing with Liam. There is something about the energy between them that unsettles me. She looks up at him like a schoolgirl with a crush. I see Nicole register it as well.

Liam's lawyer begins his questioning. His smile, meant to be encouraging reads as condescending. Emma stares at him.

Q: Good afternoon, Ms. Murphy. Can you state your full name for the record, please?

A: Emma, E-M-M-A, Murphy, M-U-R-P-H-Y.

Q: How old are you?

A: 24.

Q: You went to high school with Mr. Flynn?

A: He was a year ahead of me.

Q: So you graduated from high school in 1997?

A: Yes.

Q: You would agree you started a dating relationship [with Liam] about November 2000 and from that point forward, you began a failr regular dating relationship at least with him?

A: Yes.

Q: And that dating relationship lasted until approximately when?

A: End of December.

Q: And during the course of that relationship, you had intimate sexual relations?

A: Yes.

Q: Approximately how many occasions?

A: I would say probably twelve or thirteen.

He looks down at his notes.

Q: Between—all right. Can you tell us why you did not tell Mr. Flynn prior to June 17th that you were pregnant?

A: I tried in March, and he left where we were. I said, "I have to talk to you." And he just left.

Q: Is there any reason why you didn't try to call him?

A: I tried to call him a few times. His cousin answered the phone and always said, "Emma who?" And, "He is not here." And then I finally saw him out, and that's when I said, "I need to talk to you."

Q: And that was in March?

A: Yes.

Q: Now...

A: And that's when I found out I was pregnant, beginning of March, late February.

The questions go on like this for some time. Emma remains focused and poised.

Q: Let's go back to the evening of June 17th. At the beginning of that conversation, did you tell Liam you were pregnant?

A: Yes.

Q: And you talked for approximately how long?

A: About two hours.

Q: And what else did you tell him?

A: That I was planning to place the baby for adoption. That I was going to California so that I wouldn't have to tell my parents or my friends so it could be kept a secret.

Q: What else did you say to him that night?

A: I told him I knew that neither one of us was financially or emotionally ready for a child. I didn't want my baby bouncing back and forth from babysitter to grandparent to friends to day care centers. I wanted my baby to have an actual family. And he seemed to not agree at first and then agreed.

Q: What led you to that impression?

A: His main thing was he did not want the child to be spoiled. That's what he said, "No kid of mine is going to be spoiled." And then he said he grew up with nothing and he was fine.

Q: Did he indicate to you that he desired to raise the child himself?

A: Not at that time, no.

Q: Did he say that he wanted to be involved in the child's life in any way at that time?

A: No.

Q: Was anything else said in the course of that conversation?

A: Not too much. He said, "Okay. You made up your mind. Your mind's made up."

Q: There was a second phone conversation?

A: Yes. Even shorter than the first one. He just said, "Are you still planning on leaving?" I said, "Yes." He asked if there was anything to do to change my mind. And then he called me a "walking piece of meat with no soul."

Q: Did he use any other terms that you considered offensive?

A: He called me "irresponsible."

Q: Did he say why you were irresponsible?

A: Because I wasn't taking responsibility in raising the child myself.

Q: On April 27th, 2001, you had a sonogram confirming that you were twenty weeks pregnant. Did you see a doctor at that time?

A: It was an abortion appointment. That's why I didn't really consider it a doctor's appointment. I was going to have an abortion, and I was too far along.

Emma's frankness stops the conversation. Daniel lays his hand on my leg under the table. This is the first we have heard of her abortion plans. My vehemently pro-choice politics slams into the horror that Zelda might never have been born. Had Emma been able to follow through with her abortion I would not be sitting here today. I would not be Zelda's father.

The questions continue but I stop listening. I feel uneasy. I think about my parents and how their liberal politics were challenged by my coming out. A woman's right to choose is non-negotiable, still I offer up a silent prayer of thanks that Emma was too far along to follow through, that Zelda is alive; that I am her father.

There are always two sides to every story.

I hear Liam's lawyer asking Nicole if she has any follow-up questions. She shakes her head.

The depositions are over.

It is close to four o'clock; we have been here for six hours. Everyone looks tired, but the day is not over. We still have to hear the judge's decision regarding Liam's Habeus corpus request. If the judge sides with Liam, Zelda will fly back with Liam tomorrow.

Had I considered it a real possibility I might never have come to court. Still, I have lived with "*But if*" and "*It's not over*" for so long that my guard stays up.

Liam passes us with his lawyer in tow.

"It's insane," Daniel says, leaning into me so no one else can hear him, "that he made this request but doesn't have a single thing for her if she *does* go back with him."

We enter a courtroom. Liam and his lawyer take the table on the left and Nicole, Daniel and I sit to the right. Emma sits behind us. Once again Janet chooses to sit behind Liam. I wonder if she is sending a message to the judge.

"Why is Janet sitting over there?" I ask Nicole.

"I have no idea," she replies. "But I don't like it."

Shit.

There is no time to respond because the judge enters.

Judge Jamieson has a shock of white hair, ruddy cheeks and a gentle disposition. He wastes no time and immediately denies Liam's request; Zelda will stay with us throughout the trial. Overjoyed, I grab Daniel's leg under the table.

Liam seems unfazed by the decision. When we leave the courtroom I want to point out his ambivalence to others; instead I bite my tongue.

I do notice that Janet walks Liam to the elevator.

Nichole watches them too. "Let's hope she's not siding with him. We need her on our side."

She leans into Emma and whispers something to her before heading to the elevator herself.

When we make our way back to our car I tell Emma what a great job she did.

"I just told the truth," she says. "But can you believe he had the balls to try and take Zelda, but admitted that he had nothing for her? No bed, no food. No clothes. 'Everything's just gonna be given to me,'" she says in a fairly good imitation of Liam. Then she falls silent.

Her restraint during the depositions gives way to a raw emotional exhaustion. "It's how he gets through life." Her voice sounds sad. "Just waiting for people to take care of him."

She rolls down her window and welcomes the California air whipping around her. She closes her eyes. We ride in silence.

"What did you think about Janet?" Daniel asks. I can hear his attempt at sounding casual and wonder if Emma hears it too.

"I think Liam is an expert manipulator," she says, not missing a beat.

She asks if we could drop her at her hotel for some downtime and we readily agree. We all need time to digest today's events. We tell her we will be back in a few hours to take her out to dinner.

All I want to do upon returning home is hold Zelda and never let her go. But she is asleep.

"She's a very easy baby," Ana says and picks up her bag to leave. "She should wake up soon."

Daniel disappears into the back and I take out a pad and a pen. Winning the Habeus corpus has given me a tiny taste of hope and I latch onto it.

This is what I finally commit to paper:

Things I want to teach Zelda:

1. Put your own oxygen mask on first.
2. Own your sexuality, <u>because</u> it is exhilarating and powerful. And it belongs to you.

3. You are enough.
4. Ask for what you want. If you do not ask, you will never know.
5. Be bold.
6. Ask for help.
7. There are always two sides to every story.
8. Clear the table without being asked.
9. Never arrive empty-handed as a guest. If you are over eighteen bring a bottle of wine or flowers or a dessert, without being asked.
10. Be wary of judging if you have never walked in another's shoes.
11. Find empathy.
12. Beware of knee-jerk reactions.
13. Mistakes are good and if you make one, admit it.
14. Strip the bed when your stay as a guest is over.
15. Never intentionally hurt someone.
16. Saying sorry makes you stronger.
17. Speak out.
18. People often just want to be heard. So just listen.
19. Try.
20. Surround yourself with friends who challenge you.
21. If you find yourself in a situation where you feel unsafe (and you will), trust the instinct and get out.
22. Look people in the eye when you speak to them.
23. You are loved.
24. It is important how things begin.

23

After taking Emma out to dinner, Daniel and I collapse in front of the television. He flips aimlessly through the channels and I hardly pay attention; my mind is too busy obsessing about tomorrow's obligatory visit between Liam and Zelda. Janet has forsaken the Denny's and we are scheduled to meet Liam in the lobby of his hotel.

This morning, I had every intention of bringing Zelda and all day I insisted that I would, I *should* be the one to take her. I wanted to be with Zelda, I wanted to look Liam in the eye. But by the time Daniel turns off the television, I admit the truth.

"I can't do it," I mumble. "I know I said I would, but I can't."

"And I couldn't figure out why you kept insisting you should."

Why I love Daniel: Reason Number 1257.

Relief washes over me.

"Thank you," I say.

"Anyway, we both know how much better I am at emotionally detaching."

"I'll do both feedings then," I whisper into the dark. "At least you should be well rested."

"Happily," he agrees.

Two feedings later, I am exhausted and wired; too little sleep and too much coffee.

It is 10:45AM in the morning. Daniel left to meet Liam a half an hour ago, and I am already emotionally spent. The wait is excruciating. I wander from room to room wishing that I had gone, that I had been the one to bring her.

Sadie follows me around the house, sensing my anxiety.

"Let's get out of here," I tell her.

We are out the door, running across Melrose Avenue and into Hancock Park before I slow down. My chest heaves and even Sadie is happy to slow down.

Daniel must be with Liam by now.

I am so torn, battling what is right, what is fair, what should be. Are we meant to ignore Emma's decision? *Does* biology overrule all other considerations?

My pace picks up and my thoughts turn to Liam's sister, convinced she is the driving force behind all of this. She believes that because her brother got Emma pregnant, Zelda somehow belongs to their family.

Does she? I wonder.

Sadie jerks me to a stop.

Shit. Does she?

I have to admit that I am threatened by their blood connection. Will Zelda attach to Liam because of it?

"That's insane," I hear myself say.

It's a brief meeting, in a hotel lobby.

Pull it together.

Sadie rubs herself against my leg. "Let's go," I say and turn around, walking toward Melrose, back to our home.

At the house, I distract myself by cleaning the dishes and folding the laundry. I open the refrigerator, stare at the shelves, then close the door.

I check my email to see if Janet responded to our earlier email, then double check to make sure it actually sent. We decided that everything should be in writing for the future; even so I wince a bit at the undeniably prissy tone:

> Dear Janet,
>   We want to thank you for facilitating tomorrow's visitation. While we are not keen on inter-

acting with the birthfather, we will of course do anything to ensure Zelda's comfort. We make a concerted effort to promote her learning and development by introducing her to different environments and people appropriate for infants, so our hope is that this experience will not be jarring for her and that she will feel comfortable interacting with the birthfather. Still, we're disappointed that the birthfather did not heed the court's suggestion to send materials to familiarize Zelda with him—we do think it would've made their time together that much more pleasurable if it was a face she had at least seen in a photo or a voice she had heard on tape.

As you know, he's never asked after Zelda's health or temperament and we wish he had made an effort to find out a little about her before the meeting—perhaps knowing her favorite songs or books might've made the meeting that much more pleasant for her. Still, we have high hopes that she will rise to the occasion and demonstrate the curiosity and grace she already exhibits.

I am at a loss at what to do so I turn my frustration in her direction.

> Janet,
> Did you receive our email regarding today's visit? We never heard back from you.

Send.

Daniel's voice is in my head: never send an email when you are angry. You'll always regret it.

And I do.

I slam my computer shut and walk in circles around the house, like a trapped animal. Finally I collapse on the couch and fall asleep.

"Hello?"

A door closes. Sadie's nails click on the floor as she runs into the living room. I look at the clock; it has been two hours.

I am on my feet racing toward the front of the house before I am fully awake.

"Hi," Daniel says quietly, letting me know Zelda is asleep in her car seat. Her head leans to one side and her blanket is bunched up around her chest.

"I'm going to put her in our room," he says and heads into our room before I have a chance to greet her.

"I have to give her a kiss," I say, and follow them into the bedroom. I kiss her cheek.

Daniel looks spent as he follows me back into the den.

"Were you asleep?" he asks.

"I don't even remember falling asleep. I think I literally shut down."

We sit on the couch with the French doors open and Zelda asleep in our room.

"He is so tall," Daniel begins. "I hope Zelda gets his height."

"I need you to start from the beginning. Maybe even the parking lot."

He leans back against the sidearm of the couch.

"Wait! Before you get into the details, is there anything I need to worry about?"

"Absolutely not," he says.

Reason Number 1258.

"He's kind of sweet."

For a split second I wonder if he is kidding. But his face shows no sign of humor.

"Really?" I ask. I don't want to know if Liam is sweet so I decide not to press him further on that. "From the beginning."

"When I got there my heart was in my throat. I thought about what you would do. You're so good at defusing any situation."

"I'm not sure about that."

"It's true. It's a gift."

"It was all a little out of body. I kept saying this is insane over and over again. We were in this generic hotel lobby and Liam was sitting on this oversized baroque chair, listening to a Discman. Two things hit me: first, who listens to a Discman anymore, and then what must this be like for him. It was the first time that I put myself in his shoes, you know?"

He pauses and allows the question to sit there, unanswered.

"Go on," I say and clench my jaw. I don't want to feel empathetic toward Liam.

"Liam saw me and got out of the chair and gave me a little

wave. All I could think was he's just a kid himself. But once he started walking toward me all I could think was he's *really* tall. Isn't that crazy? I am meeting Zelda's birthfather and all I can think about is his height."

Daniel rubs his eyes.

"What was he wearing?"

"Um..." I see him search his memory. "Jeans...a t-shirt? He led me to this smaller room off the main lobby where we sat down on a couch in the middle of the room. There was a man in the corner reading a book, totally oblivious to us."

We watch Sadie get up, circle her spot and then lay herself back down.

"Then it struck me that no one had ever introduced us, so I said, "I'm Daniel by the way." And he said, 'So the other guy is Ben?'"

"What?" I laugh.

"Right? The other guy."

"I would like to be referred to as The Other Guy from now on," I say.

Daniel smiles for a moment and I can see him relive the moment.

"His tone took me by surprise. He wasn't trying to be rude or funny, no one bothered to tell him, but somehow just telling him my name made it better. I did a Ben."

I smile, embarrassed by all the hatefulness I had chosen to direct at this stranger.

"He's a kid," Daniel says. "That's what I kept thinking. He's just a kid. It was also clear that no one told him how this visit was meant to go either. Zelda was really into the patterns on the floor that the light made as it poured in through the large windows, so Liam and I just sat there for a moment. I was trying to figure out what to do, so then I handed Zelda to Liam. I needed to get on with it. I made it a kind of game at first so she wouldn't flip out. Then I pushed his Virgin plastic bag with the stuffed animal along with our diaper bag toward his feet and stood up. He looked petrified and I kind of liked that. I didn't want to hang out with him and honestly," he stops for a second, "I didn't want to make this easy for him. Is that bad?"

"No."

"I grabbed *The New Yorker* from the diaper bag and walked away before he could say anything. I knew he wanted me to stay and I worried that if he asked me to my face I wouldn't be able to say no. But as I walked away I heard him say, 'you can stay here if you want' but I just kept walking."

Daniel's face falls as though he is unable to fully shake his own guilt.

"I needed him to see how hard it is to take care of a small child and I knew my presence would relax Zelda and give him something to play off of, so instead I sat across the room and watched them over my magazine. For a while, he just sat there with her on his lap, saying nothing, and I wondered how long she would be okay with that. Finally, he reached down and took the stuffed animal out of the bag and said something to her. I couldn't hear him. She reached out to touch it but then I thought I saw her look around for me. It took everything in me not to jump up and grab her. But I didn't and really, he was kind of dorkily sweet with her. Awkward and anxious but he was trying."

I can feel myself heating up.

You weren't there. Just listen.

"I loved her so much in that moment; for being so awesome, for not fussing, for being independent. I could see his lips move again. Then the man in the corner got up and walked out of the room and we watched him leave. I was struck by Liam's Midwestern look; it's funny to think about us having a tall, blond Irish child. Liam must have felt me staring at him because he glanced over at me from across the room and I pretended not to see him. Like I was spacing out. He looked frightened and it broke my heart."

Daniel sighs.

"He found the book you keep in the diaper bag. The one where each page has a different fabric or material to touch and he flipped through the pages."

"She loves that book," I say.

"Then he stood up and walked toward me, and I knew I couldn't avoid him, so I put the magazine down and smiled at him. I had no idea what to say, so I talked to Zelda. He asked me to hold her and then walked back to his seat and gathered up the bags and while his back was turned, I told her how much I loved her and then I told her how much Papa loves her."

I do love you.

"He walked back to me holding the bags and a disposable camera and asked if he could take a few pictures."

"What did you say?"

"I said, "Of course." Let his family see how happy and healthy she is. He did ask if I could get her to smile and I tried but halfheartedly. I was really self-conscious about being in the pictures though, so I kept my face down. Then I asked him if he wanted a photo with the two of them and it was almost like he hadn't thought about it."

"Did you ever want to just ask him why he was doing all this?"

"Yes, of course. But I couldn't. I knew that I could make this whole thing easier on him, help the conversation along, but I couldn't. Or maybe I just wouldn't. It took everything in me to stay seated across from him. I mean he is holding our lives hostage, trying to take our child." Daniel's eyes grow distant before he adds; "I didn't want to make anything easy for him."

It feels good to hear some anger in his voice. I am on my feet pacing the living room. I need to move. Daniel watches me for a minute and then says, "I need you to sit down."

I do, my foot bouncing.

"He asked me how she slept at night and I realized that with every question he asked, I was trying to suss out what he wants, or why he's asking. Do I tell him that she is a good sleeper, so he sees how at peace she is, or do I say she's a bad sleeper, to scare him off? But in that moment, I hated who I was being with him. He really is just a kid; he showed no ill intent. He was just trying to make conversation and I wasn't helping him out at all. I thought about what Emma had said and I just told him the truth. I told him that she slept pretty well and left it at that. He mentioned how beautiful her eyes were and then laughed and added that he hoped Zelda didn't get his eyebrows, because then they would "stretch clear across her face." I laughed with him and for the briefest flash I was okay sitting with this guy. He was still holding Zelda on his lap and she kind of wobbled a bit and he made a joke about her not putting her foot "there, as it would hurt" and I thought after all the depositions I really didn't want to think about this man's penis anymore. He mentioned how much happier Zelda was today than she was at Denny's and I got really embarrassed."

"Not one of my finer moments," I say.

"Either of ours," he shrugs. "Zelda began to squirm and I could feel his tension spike and without a word he handed her to me.

Part of me wanted to leave her in his arms so he would be forced to deal with a restless baby but I took her. I was so happy to have her back that for a moment I forgot about Liam. He stood up and declared that he should go pack and I didn't argue, even though I knew his flight didn't leave for hours. I didn't care. I asked him if he would like to hold her again but he didn't. I wanted to be clear that he was ending our visit, and not me, and then we stood there for what felt like a minute, in silence. That is when I thought about asking him why he was doing this. It seemed so clear that he was not connected to Zelda. Nor did he really want to be. Obviously I couldn't ask. I don't even know if he could have answered the question, really. He stepped away and thanked me several times for taking the time to bring her and I wished him a safe flight. I can't tell you how happy I was to step out of that hotel with Zelda in my arms. I kept saying, 'Let's go home.'"

"I'm proud of you."

"I'm not done," he says. There is a sudden edge to his voice. "I strapped Zelda into her car seat and reached into the diaper bag for my keys and found a carefully folded fifty dollar bill. Liam must have slipped it into the bag when he went to get his camera. For a second I wondered if he did it because his lawyer told him to or just because he wanted to. I thought about how many hours he needed to work for fifty dollars. And then I was sitting in the parking lot and I suddenly started to cry. Like uncontrollably sob."

We sit together for a minute in silence.

"I don't know what to say."

"There is nothing to say," he says. "It's fine. I'm fine." He stands up and adds, "I need to lie down."

Left alone, I feel embarrassed that I called Liam The Devil, embarrassed that I never *really* thought about his side of the story. I am uncomfortable at how easily I was able to demonize the unknown. Plenty of people don't like me because I am gay and like me less because I am a gay father—I resent them for their judgment. My behavior has been no better. Liam is not the devil. He is a twenty-five-year-old kid who is convinced he is doing the right thing.

Zelda is awake. I can hear her babbling full voice from our room. Our door opens and Daniel walks over to me with Zelda in his arms.

"Look who's here?" he says to Zelda. "It's Papa."

"I got her. I know you need to sleep," I say.

"Thanks."

Zelda reaches for me.

"I think someone wants to see you," he adds.

I take her into my arms and kiss her over and over again.

24

January ends and Daniel and I celebrate Valentine's Day at home with sushi and sake.

Toward the end of February, with the trial fast approaching, Daniel and I call Nicole three weeks out to discuss a settlement offer. We have no interest in keeping Liam out of Zelda's life and believe that if we offer him an "out," he may just take it. Nicole is open to the idea and suggests we write out our offer so she can take it to his lawyer.

We speak with Emma and I ask if she ever runs into Liam.

"No, thank God," she laughs.

I think about this all the time, the two of them co-existing in this small town, sharing this unspoken history.

"Has he gotten in touch with you guys?" There is definite anxiety in her voice.

"Nope."

"What a shock," she says, with evident relief.

Liam has not reached out to us at all.

"We're trying to see if Liam will settle out of court. If we promise him visits and whatnot."

"Never," she says without a moment's hesitation. "Why would he?"

She is right and yet still I hope.

We email Emma her flight information so she can come for the trial.

Two weeks become ten days.

We email Nicole our offer:

- The birthfather will have the right to visit with the child three periods each year.

- The adoptive parents agree to pay for the birthfather's airfare for each third visit, provided that a twelve-month period has not elapsed with the birthfather failing to visit.

- If the birthfather fails to exercise any visit within any twelve-month period, any further contact between the birthfather and the child shall be in the sole discretion of the adoptive parents.

- During the first twelve-month period and following the first two visits by the birthfather, the adoptive parents agree to bring the child to Minnesota for a three-day weekend visit in order for her to visit her paternal biological relatives.

- The birthfather agrees not to disclose to the birthmother's family the fact that she was pregnant and gave birth to this child. Neither party shall disparage the other in the presence of the minor.

- The birthfather shall be allowed to call and write to the child and send presents.

Nicole believes we have been more than fair. She sends our offer to Liam's lawyer.

Ten days become seven which become six which become five.

Our pediatrician tells me that Zelda is in the top twenty percent for height. "You are going to have a tall one," he laughs.

Five becomes four.

Sadie curls up around Zelda's bassinet when she naps in it. She is a herding breed; even she knows that Zelda is part of the family.

Three.

The moon is hidden behind clouds and the night is cold. Daniel is in his office working on a script that is due the following week. He buries himself deep inside a world where he is the creator of all, a world that he controls. My distraction is Zelda; his is his work, but my distraction is asleep and I am alone.

The trial is three days away and my pretense of strength begins to erode.

I cannot protect Zelda.

I cannot protect you from everything.

I break down.

I have been holding on so tightly, too tightly. Once again, the release feels good. I force myself to sit with the knowledge that Zelda may be taken from me and there is nothing I can do about it.

I might lose my daughter.

It feels better to admit it.

My breathing slows. There is stillness, and then a deep sense of calm. The truth makes reality easier to accept. I crawl into bed, happy to be next to Zelda. I fall asleep.

Two days before the trial, we receive a FedEx package from Nicole containing our brief.

Daniel emerges from his office.

I nod.

We sit down at the dining room table and turn to the first page where a Post-it note reads: *Have not heard anything regarding your offer. Sorry, Nicole.*

Trial Brief on Petition to Determine Parental
Rights of Alleged Natural Father Liam Flynn,
Pursuant to Family Code Section 7662/7664
Date: March 7, 2002
Time: 1:30 PM
Dept: 421

A. Overview of the case: Before this court is a petition to terminate the parental rights of LIAM FLYNN under the "best interest" standard of Family Code section 7664 so that BENJAMIN [not really my name, just Ben, never has been Benjamin] SCHWARTZ and DANIEL BERNSTEIN may complete their adoption of ZELDA, who is almost six months old [tomorrow actually] and has been in their home since her birth last September 8 to EMMA MUR-PHY.

Daniel and I both look at one another.
"This is fucking crazy."
"Crazy," he echoes and we continue to read.

If the adoption fails, the adoptive parents will argue that they must be named as her guardian because she will suffer detriment from being removed from their care (Adoption of Danielle G. 2001; Guardianship of Zachary H. 1999.)

Mr. Flynn will probably claim that he should be given the rights of a presumed father, as defined by the California Supreme Court in Adoption of Kelsey S. (1992), which allows a non-marital father, like Mr. Flynn, to nevertheless have the same right to block an adoption as he would have if he were married to the birthmother if he can establish that:

[o]nce he knows or reasonably should know of the pregnancy, he must promptly attempt to assume his parental responsibilities as fully as the mother will allow and his circumstances permit. In particular, the father must demonstrate 'a willingness himself to assume full custody of the child – not merely to block adoption by others.' A court should also consider the father's public acknowledgment of paternity, payment of pregnancy and birth expenses commensurate with his ability to do so, and prompt legal action to seek custody of the child."

His argument must fail. Mr. Flynn will admit that he provided no financial or emotional support to Ms. Murphy during her pregnancy. He will admit that he told her that he did not oppose her adoption plan shortly after she told him she was pregnant and that after that time he never told Ms. Murphy or any other person connected with the adoption that he opposed the adoption until after the baby was born and placed with the Petitioners. He will further admit that he did not even decide to try to block the adoption until after the baby was born.

"That seems positive," Daniel says not looking up from the page.

"Give me a second," I say. He is a faster reader than me. He gets up and goes into the kitchen, allowing me time to catch up.

"It does seem good," I say, as he walks back into the dining room with a plate full of orange slices. I can't eat as my stomach is in my throat. "I mean he didn't do any of that."

"I honestly don't understand what his case is," he says.

Twelve pages lay out the "Posture of the case," a basic time line of legal events throughout the pregnancy, followed by a section called "Parties," which lays out all four players, who we are, our ages, jobs, and who represents us. Next is the "Anticipated Testimony of the Birth Parents;" this is a detailed summary of their depositions. Nicole goes on and lays out a "Legal Framework" for why Liam's rights should be terminated and the adoption should be allowed to proceed. On page 20 lies the answer to my initial question:

Zelda is almost six months old, and has been with the adoptive parents all her life. She has her own independent right to a secure and stable home.

Where a child has formed familial bonds with a de facto family with whom the child was placed owing to biological parents unfitness (In re Jasmon O.) or initial failure to establish a parent-child relationship (Lehr v. Robertson, supra, Adoption of Michael H, supra) and where it is shown that the child would be harmed by any severance of those bonds, the child's constitutionally protected interests outweigh those of the biological parents... California recognizes the principle that children are not merely chattels belonging to their parents, but rather have fundamental interests of their own. The California Supreme Court has determined that custody does not automatically flow from parental rights.

"I fucking love California," I say. We turn back to the brief. Our house is eerily quiet, our focus so intense that everything else has receded except for the sound of paper being turned.

In her conclusion, Nicole states that The California Supreme Court squarely places the burden of assuming responsibility on the man who is seeking to assert his rights, and disallows all excuses.

...Men on this planet for several million years have with impunity planted their seeds and then moved on...[I]f you have sexual intercourse with a woman of childbearing years...you have good cause to believe that you may have just created a human being...So you as a male human being, if you want to protect your rights as a father, [have] got to keep in touch...if you don't keep in touch with a woman with whom you have had intercourse, then you're putting yourself at risk to be a day late and a dollar short...The glimmer starts and your responsibility begins when you have intercourse with her...[I]f you are really a sincere guy and you want to put on the cloak of fatherhood, then you should have run down here, not walked...Your choice, your strategy, but you burned up maybe five months of time that would have made you look a lot better.

"Makes sense, though," Daniel says turning onto the final page of the brief. "I mean, it takes two."

Nicole concludes: Mr. Flynn had sex with a woman of childbearing years, and failed to use protection on several occasions. He did not even think about her becoming pregnant. He learned of her pregnancy in June 2001, yet he did not keep in touch with her. After the child was born, he did not visit with her, or ask to do so, until she was almost five months old. He allowed everyone else to assume his responsibilities. The duty was <u>his</u> to stay in touch with her and to demonstrate his full commitment to her child. <u>Michael H.</u> is even clearer, and <u>dispositive</u>: No matter how "diligent" Mr. Flynn now looks by his coming forward asking for custody, his actions have come at the wrong time.

The adoptive parents respectfully request that this court finds that Mr. Flynn's consent to the adoption is not necessary because he acted too late, and to terminate his parental rights and allow this adoption to proceed.

Respectfully submitted, Nicole A. Morgan

Daniel and I both lean back in our chairs. Nicole has laid out a beautiful, succinct argument.

And yet.

25

It is just before three in the morning. It is March and our trial begins in less than twelve hours. A wind whips itself around our house. A branch scratches itself against one of the windows—the sound unsettles me even more. *Tap scratch tap, tap scratch tap.* My mind wanders to Liam and Emma asleep in separate hotel rooms in Los Angeles. I wonder if they lie awake too. Never in their wildest dreams could they have imagined themselves in this city, in this situation.

My thoughts are a jumbled mess. I am confident but uncertain. I am secure and terrified. I am at peace and I am torn up. In her sleep, Zelda makes a noise that sounds like a laugh. I watch her for a while; I will always be here for you, I think. No matter what happens.

She makes another noise and I wonder what she dreams about. She devoured her two o'clock bottle and grows longer and leaner with every day.

Tap scratch tap. The day is here.

It is almost four in the morning. The warmth of Daniel's sleeping body comforts me and I gently lay my hand on his arm. I am proud of us, of how well we have weathered this storm so far.

"Are you awake?" he asks.

I flip back over and can just make out his face.

"I'm freaking out," he whispers.

Just listen.

"I don't know what I'll do if she's taken from us."

"We are going to be okay," I whisper back into the dark.

"Are we?"

He wants to believe so much.

I don't clarify my answer, because I am not certain what question I am answering. If Zelda will remain ours, or if Daniel and I will be okay.

When my eyes open, the room is brighter. I sit up.

Who am I kidding? Zelda is my daughter.

Daniel opens our bedroom door and climbs back into bed.

"You're a remarkable father," he says. "We have to get ready."

When I turn off the shower, I am met with the sound of Zelda's laughter ricocheting through the house, and I need to be a part of it. She is on Daniel's stomach, her small arms pressing herself away from his face.

"I have *no* idea what she finds so funny," he says, joining her laughter, "but I am loving her right now."

Remember this, I think.

Still wet, I flop onto the bed and give into the joy.

Zelda rolls off Daniel and finds herself between us. She looks at me and then at Daniel. She is discovering a new game, I can see it dawn upon her. She turns her head back and forth between us while a crooked smile spreads across her face. We are not privy to the rules of her game but whatever it is she is owning it. I lean over and blow a raspberry on her stomach causing her to belly laugh.

Daniel stands, "Time to get dressed."

Zelda rolls over. She has just begun to try to push herself up to a seated position.

Stepping into a pair of black pants, Daniel says, "She's getting pretty good at that."

And then there she is, sitting up by herself. Her eyes widen in joyous surprise. Then she face plants onto our quilt. Daniel and I leap onto the bed and congratulate her on this major accomplishment.

I shake off an image that flashes before me. Ten years from

now, Daniel and I on our patio, childless. He asks me if I remember the day Zelda sat up for the first time.

Stop.

"You did it," I say and push the darkness away. "You sat up!" I kiss her face over and over again. "Now tell me, smart girl, what should I wear to the very first day of my very first custody hearing?"

Daniel shakes his head and lifts Zelda off the bed. As he leaves the room, I note that he has put on a tie. He looks handsome.

Left alone, I am once again standing in my underwear trying to decide what to wear before picking up Emma. The first time she was seven and a half months pregnant and 9/11 hadn't happened yet. Then I was excited, filled with the unknown thrill of it all. Today my feelings are much more complicated.

I pull on a pair of khakis and a light blue button-down shirt.

"Like any other day," I say out loud as I walk into the kitchen and realize that I am speaking to myself. Daniel is in the yard with Zelda picking lemons.

I watch them together. Daniel talks nonstop and I can only imagine what he is telling her about. I lean out into the yard and say, "I want to feed her before we go."

Five minutes later she is in her high chair, mouth open in anticipation of her jar of carrots. The lid pops open and her tongue shoots out as she awaits the first bite. She is obsessed with carrots. She can't get enough of them.

Daniel leans down and kisses Zelda's head. "I'm going to call Nicole and tell her we are putting a clock on our offer to Liam."

"Excellent." I say. "Tell her once we walk into that courtroom the offer is off the table."

Daniel takes the call outside. I can't make out what he says but the call is brief.

"What is *wrong* with her?" he demands as he reenters the dining room. Zelda is now halfway through a jar of apples. "Nicole said Janet told Liam his case was 'strong.'"

"Does Janet know something we don't?"

"No," Daniel says, with such force that Zelda looks at me, startled. She looks like she could burst into tears. "Sorry, sweet girl," Daniel says stroking the top of her head. "Look, apples!" I add, but my tone sounds false, even to me.

"Nicole disagrees but won't say it flat out."

We are left to wonder whether people around us are painting a rosier picture than truly exists, if there is some part of our case that is weaker than we suspect. We read Nicole's brief, Liam's case seems shaky at best. But if that is true, why did Janet tell Liam his case was strong?

"We need to get Emma," Daniel says, after a moment. "And I told Nicole that our offer is pulled as soon as we walk into that courtroom."

"Damn right," I say, wiping Zelda's mouth. Unstrapped from her highchair, I drop the filthy tray into the kitchen sink before I take her into our bedroom to change her diaper.

The front door opens. "Hello?" Ana has arrived.

"Hi," I say. "We're in here."

Zelda twists her body toward the sound of Ana's voice.

"We should go," Daniel says and lifts Zelda into his arms. I grab a tie.

Daniel hands Zelda to Ana. I intercept her and give her one last good-bye. "Bye, sweet girl," I say and bury my face in her neck.

Will you understand why we fought this hard?

"I love you so much," I whisper. The words get caught in my throat. I hand her to Ana.

"We'll be back later this afternoon," I say and walk quickly out of the house.

Emma doesn't see us as we pull up. She is in a black skirt and a green button-down shirt. Even from within the car, I sense her calm and find myself wanting to latch onto it.

"Morning," she says, stepping into the car.

"Did you sleep all right?" Daniel asks, as I simultaneously tell Emma how pretty she looks.

"Yes, I did and thank you," she says picking up on our anxiety. "I'm glad I can be here."

I swallow.

Keep it together, I tell myself.

"Nicole said she sent some questions for me?"

"Yes. I have them," I say, and hand her a stack of pages. "They're pretty straightforward."

Nicole sent a list of trial questions for all three of us. Daniel and I went over ours last night and Emma will go over hers at breakfast.

We grab a table by the window in The Griddle, a hipster breakfast place on Sunset Boulevard. Emma flips through her fifteen pages of questions.

Daniel asks Emma if she would like something to drink.

"Orange juice, please," she says without looking up, "and coffee."

The waitress appears and Daniel orders us all drinks.

Emma looks up from the list. "These questions are basically the same ones from the depositions. When did Liam and I meet? Did Liam ever offer me money?" She flips through several pages. "Did he ever let me know he wanted to raise the child?" She belly laughs. "I got this."

The waitress returns with our coffee and takes our order.

"What is your wish for the baby's custody now?" Emma reads and then teases us with a silence. "I want her to stay where she is," she says and smiles broadly, clearly enjoying us. "With her parents."

Daniel and I smile.

"Do you want to go over them?" Daniel asks knowing full well she doesn't need our help. We need hers. But Nicole told us to ask, so we ask.

"I'm good."

"No doubt," Daniel says.

Once again she doesn't ask about Zelda and we take our lead from her. She eats her pancakes as Daniel and I pick at ours. The few bites I manage to get down feel like lead in my stomach.

An hour later, we drive into the courthouse parking structure. As we spiral up the ramps, I am reminded of the day we left the hospital with Zelda. She was one day old and I was convinced that my life was changed forever, but now, as we pass level three, I understand that life is full of what we achingly want to believe are "forever changes."

"Let's do this," Emma says as Daniel pulls into a spot.

26

We make our way across the vast lobby of the courthouse and I note the time on the large clock above the elevators. It is just before one in the afternoon on March 7th. Tomorrow Zelda will be six months old.

The elevator lets us out on the third floor. I scan the large, open space and see we are once again the first to arrive.

"That's a lot of purple," I mutter and hear Emma laugh. The large open waiting area is almost entirely purple; purple carpet, tables, and chairs.

It reminds me of a Chuck E. Cheese restaurant without the food. The wall-to-wall carpeting is worn in places, and plastic chairs line three of the four walls; overhead televisions are mounted throughout the room, soundlessly playing cartoons. In a corner a young couple sits huddled together, a car seat at their feet. Wooden doors line one wall, each leading to its own courtroom. There is no noise, only an impenetrable silence that seems soaked into the carpet.

I walk away, ostensibly to look out the window, but really to gather myself.

Daniel laughs and I turn around to see Emma leaning into him. He catches my eye from across the room and I marvel at how good the world can be. How a quiet, self-contained, stoic woman from the Midwest could end up placing her child with two talky, intellectualizing, neurotic men in Southern California. It might just be the definition of a miracle.

"Do you need anything?" I ask Emma as I join them. "Some water? A soda?"

"I'm okay," she says and I am reminded that she is always "okay." When we first met, her constant stream of "okays" frustrated me. As someone who has learned to ask for what I want, I found her tentative, non-declarative demeanor infuriating. But then I realized that most of the time she honestly is "okay."

Jonathan Ross arrives and wraps Emma in a bear hug. His suit and tie underscores the seriousness of the proceedings. He tells her how beautiful she is and I flash to a conversation we had had three months earlier.

"I am a facilitator, a bridge," he had told Daniel and me when we were planning for the first hearing in Minnesota. "A birthmother calls me because the child she is carrying is meant to be with a family I represent. I create the bridge to connect them. It is already meant to be."

Jonathan pulls out a pack of cards from his briefcase.

"Would you like to see a trick?"

I am grateful for the distraction, for the thoughtfulness behind this gesture. He reveals that he occasionally moonlights as a magician at the Magic Castle in Los Angeles, yet another surprise from the man I initially dismissed for his "I like to win" comment. Now I count my blessings that we have him on our side.

His trick dumbfounds us. We beg to know how he does it but in true magician-slash-lawyer style, he refuses to divulge the secret.

Nicole arrives, wearing a black pantsuit and carrying her briefcase. "No word on your offer," she says immediately. "Not so smart on his part if you ask me. You were extremely generous."

She asks Emma if she needs any help with the questions.

"I'm good," Emma responds. I think I see a flash of irritation and I wonder if it's because we all keep asking her the same question.

"Great." Nicole nods. "Then I'm going to go ahead and get myself situated."

She heads off to a small table where she takes a stack of paperwork from her briefcase. Jonathan joins her just as Liam lopes in, wearing jeans and an untucked white button-down shirt; the role of the bad guy hanging on him half-heartedly, like a shirt two sizes too large.

I look at Emma, who looks at Liam, and I see disappointment in her eyes. Disappointment in Liam, in the system, in the fact that life has brought them to this point. Something else catches her eye; she sits up straight.

"Who the hell are they?" Emma asks.

Two young women follow Liam. They head straight across the large room, and sit by a window. The two women turn to each other and begin to whisper. Liam looks out the window, everything about him is unreadable.

"Who are they?" Emma asks Nicole, as she walks over to us.

"Evidently he brought character witnesses."

"I have never seen them before," Emma says, now shaken.

No one knows what to say.

Emma drops into her chair. On top of everything else she now has to deal with two additional, potential local gossips.

"The judge is running late," Jonathan, informs us. "And don't worry about them," he adds, barely glancing back across the room. "It's just another perk of our California system. We actually pay for them to come so he can never claim he wasn't given a completely fair shot."

"Wait," I say, my voice hushed but harsh, "the cost of *their* travel is covered, too?"

Jonathan nods. My anger is immediate. I excuse myself before I say something I might regret and hurry into the bathroom where I grip the edge of the sink. A hard, ugly anger is reflected back at me in the mirror and I relish it. I like it when fear and rage coexist. Still, I must stay in control; the trial has not even begun.

Think about Zelda, I tell myself. Think about her laughing this morning. Think about her asleep, think about her breath, and think about one little arm up above her head as she sleeps.

Every night, before I fall asleep, I stand over her and kiss the palm of my hand. Then I hold my hand just above her sleeping head. "You are enough," I say to myself silently. "You are worthwhile," comes next as my hand begins to move in small circles above her heart, "and I wish you an open heart." Then my hand travels down the length of her body and back up before I bend down and kiss the top of her head. "I love you," I whisper. I always end with that. "I love you." Only then can I sleep.

The anger that overwhelmed me a minute ago dissipates. I am ready to join the others.

"You good?" Daniel asks when I sit down next to him.

"I am," I tell him.

The room has filled up. We are not the only ones whose lives will be changed today.

Janet hustles in with a frazzled air, holding tightly to her oversized black bag. She makes her way across the room to Liam, confirming my worst suspicions.

The room that moments ago felt large and open now feels stifling and claustrophobic. Every minute moves with excruciating slowness.

"Liam's lawyer never submitted a brief?" I ask Jonathan.

Jonathan shakes his head. "It's unusual but he told us he was fine with just Nicole's."

This seems irresponsible but must bode well for us. Unless, of course, it means our case is hopeless and he doesn't even need to explain it.

The judge remains behind schedule. It is now almost three o'-clock.

"I'm going to check on Zelda," I tell Daniel and slip away. It's too hard for me to stay still.

"Stay close by," Daniel says, always the optimist.

I am back at the windows that look out onto the distant San Gabriel Mountains. Three people are huddled together outside the building, smoking cigarettes and laughing.

I resent their joy.

Ana tells me she and Zelda just returned from a long walk around the neighborhood, that she ate a big lunch and is now asleep.

"We may be home before she wakes up but if not give her a kiss for me," I tell her before I hang up.

By 3:40 we are all drained by waiting in this airless room for over two and a half hours. Emma is in the bathroom. Jonathan has put his cards away and Nicole is on a call.

Daniel leans in and murmurs, "I'm losing my mind."

"Me, too. And all I can think about is about *Kramer vs. Kramer.*"

Daniel nods. "'I was thinking about Billy waking up in his room with his little clouds. Clouds all around that I painted....'"

I laugh.

At four o'clock, one of the courtroom doors opens and a balding bailiff walks out. A jolt runs through the dead space. He approaches Liam and his lawyer who stand. Without looking at us, the three of them disappear into the judge's chamber.

"What just happened?" Daniel asks.

"I don't know," Jonathan responds.

"Shouldn't we be included in whatever is being discussed about our daughter?" I ask, not bothering to hide my animosity. I turn on Nicole. "Do you have any idea what's happening?"

"The judge wanted to speak with Liam," she says and I want to strangle her.

Seriously?

I turn to Daniel, "How do they not know what is happening?"

"I hope he's getting a good talking to," Emma says. I laugh anxiously.

Twenty minutes later, the door opens and we are all back on our feet. Liam emerges, his eyes fixed on the ground.

Was Emma right? Did Liam get a talking to?

His lawyer waves Nicole over.

"Let's see what's going on," Nicole says. Her tone tells us that we are to stay put.

My knees have gone weak,

The two of them meet in the middle of the room. The trajectory of my life is being determined before my eyes and I am a witness. I can't hear any of the conversation.

Nicole turns around and heads toward us.

Is that a smile?

Daniel takes hold of my hand.

"Liam dropped his case," she says as she reaches us. "He will accept your offer if it still stands and is ready to sign over his rights."

Suddenly everyone is hugging. Daniel hugs me. I hug Emma and Jonathan slaps me on the back. I look across the room at Liam whose expression reveals nothing.

Shouldn't something else happen? Shouldn't he apologize? Shouldn't I be yelling or crying or jumping up and down?

Instead, I am numb. I haven't swallowed and when I do I almost choke.

Just like that it is all over.

All I want is Zelda.

You are ours.

We had no idea how long this trial might last but with one conversation behind closed doors Liam ended it. Just like he started it. One day he was a threat and now he isn't. It's difficult not to feel jilted, as though we were not given our day in court. Like Liam got off too easily.

But that's crazy, right?

"Liam *did* ask if he could name Zelda," Nicole says, hesitantly.

I freeze, shocked. He wants to name her?

"She has a name," Daniel says, not missing a beat.

We don't need to fight anymore, I think.

"Can we have a minute?" I take Daniel away from everyone else.

"It's over," I say.

"Yes."

"No," I repeat, allowing our new reality to sink in. "It's over." He looks at me. "This is a good thing for Zelda. We never wanted to keep her birth parents out of her life. She is ours now. But without them..." I allow my words to trail off.

"Perhaps he could give her a middle name," he suggests, "an additional middle name."

"Yes. But then I want to ask Emma, too," I add.

"Definitely."

Before we agree to Liam's request we pull Emma aside.

We explain his request, and then ask if she'd be willing to give Zelda a middle name too.

"I would love to," Emma says and beams.

Zelda's given middle name is Regenbogen, from Daniel's side. His great-great-grandfather escaped the pogroms, arriving at the Polish border after a major rainstorm. When the soldiers asked for his name, he knew he couldn't give his real (Jewish) name. He looked up in the sky where a rainbow had just appeared. "Regenbogen," he said.

Liam chooses Malia, a name he had always loved. Emma chooses Lynn, her middle name.

Zelda Malia Lynn Regenbogen Barnz.

We offer Liam a visit with Zelda before he leaves the next day, then Daniel, Emma and I drive away from the courthouse for the last time.

There are no words to describe what it felt like to hold you in my arms when we returned home that day. There is only a feeling I will never forget.

Daniel and I call our families to share the news.

Ana goes home for a few hours; we want to take Emma out for a final celebratory dinner so she will come back. Daniel reads Zelda a book in the den while she drinks a bottle. I sit just outside on the patio and listen.

After dinner, when we drop Emma off at her hotel, she stops herself before closing her door.

"Can you pick me up a little earlier tomorrow morning?" she asks. "I'd like to see Zelda."

"Of course," we say. "Of course."

I sleep deeply.

At ten the next morning I walk with Zelda to meet Liam.

"Hey Liam," I say, as he walks over to me. He has brought his friends with him. "I'm Ben. The other one," I joke and wonder if he gets the reference. He laughs.

"Nice to meet you," he says.

He takes Zelda and immediately joins the young women across the room. I watch them as they negotiate Zelda. She is well rested and content. His friends spend most of their time talking to each other and Liam holds Zelda on his lap and listens.

A half hour later he returns and stands over me.

"Well," he says, "we have to head out. Thanks for bringing her."

"Happy to," I say.

And I am.

I think about Daniel's visit in the hotel lobby and how different things are today.

We shake hands and they leave.

Zelda and I walk back to our house.

Daniel is not home. He went to pick up Emma. I feel badly that Zelda has fallen asleep and wonder if I should wake her up. Then the door opens and Emma walks in.

"Hi," I say and give her a hug. "She fell asleep. I'm so sorry. She should be up soon."

"How was Liam?" she asks.

"He was fine, really. He was nice and it was brief."

Emma's eyes roll. She is not ready to forgive him and I can't blame her.

"Should we go see her?" I ask and she nods without the least bit of apprehension.

Emma is just behind me when I turn the knob and walk into the bedroom. Zelda sleeps in a pale blue t-shirt.

"I am happy to wake her up," I whisper as we stand next to the bed. I watch Emma set eyes on her biological child for the first time.

"Don't," she murmurs. Her eyes remain fixed on Zelda. She stands perfectly still, her head just tilted to one side.

You are asleep in your crib, and your right hand clenches a blanket I made for you. Your left leg pokes through, fat and beautiful. Like always, your left arm lies above your head. I watch Emma watch you, for a long time. She doesn't ask to hold you—perhaps because you are asleep, perhaps because she is not ready—but she is there, fully present. She knows you are safe, that you are loved, that you are forever where you belong. She closes her eyes for a moment. When she opens them she looks at you with the gentlest of smiles. In that moment she lets go, I am sure of it.

"I wanted to see her," she whispers. And she turns to leave.

27

"Hello?" Daniel says loudly enough to quiet down the fifty or so friends who have gathered in our backyard.

It is September 8, 2002, Zelda's first birthday. We are hosting an over-the-top party to celebrate her birth and the end of our legal nightmare.

It is a beautiful, this-is-why-we-live-in-Los Angeles kind of day and the bluegrass band we hired stops playing. The same band plays the Sunday Hollywood Farmers' Market and Zelda loves them.

"We want to thank you all so much for coming," Daniel says. The guests begin to make their way over to us. "This party has been a long time coming," he says, to cheers and applause. "And it's actually many celebrations in one."

As I hold Zelda, Daniel turns to me, his joy infectious.

"Today we are celebrating a lot," he says. "Zelda's birthday, of course, but it's also a baby shower, an adoption finalization and a baby-naming all in one. Most of you know we went through a challenging time, and we promised ourselves that if we got through it, we'd have a blow-out party."

There is a palpable feeling of elation. I feel a deep sense of gratitude for these friends, for Emma, for Daniel and for Zelda, always Zelda.

A late afternoon light bathes the yard and I flash back to our room at Good Samaritan Hospital, when Zelda was one day old and we had just finished giving her her first bath. The same light filled the room then.

"In the spirit of naming," Daniel continues, "we wanted to say a few words about names and weather." Daniel turns to me and addresses Zelda. "Zelda, one of your middle names, Regenbogen, comes from your great grandmother and her sisters, the Regenbogen sisters. We wish you a life like their lives. They lived long and prosperously, they were marvelous women who partied and sang and told stories. They traveled, and saw plays and concerts and swam well into their nineties, one even eloped in her seventies. That same Regenbogen, Freda, threw herself birthday parties every year until she died, and there was always plenty of scotch."

Guests raise their glasses, someone calls out, "Hear, hear."

"Your last name Barnz is a combination of Schwartz and Bernstein and we, too, have a little thing with weather. When Schwartz asked Bernstein to spend the rest of his life with him, it was raining in Siena. We had taken refuge in a beautiful old library, and when Bernstein said yes, and we floated outside, the skies had cleared and the sun was shining and the church bells were ringing. That's part one. Part two came when we had our commitment ceremony and Hurricane Floyd practically wiped out the eastern seaboard. But as fate or God would have it, the morning of the festivities dawned bright and clear. And twenty-four hours after you were born, dear Zelda, an earthquake hit Los Angeles, and that was a sign that you were in the right family."

The whole party is now silent.

"We then got caught in a different kind of storm, and there were points where it looked very bleak for us. We should've known that the same God or fate that had seen fit for a strong, beautiful blond-haired, blue-eyed, Irish-Catholic woman from Minnesota to choose two brown-haired, brown-eyed men from L.A. to raise her child would see us out of that storm. And sure enough, we survived that storm, and we are overjoyed to be here today, so proud to be your fathers."

Daniel turns and takes in the sight of everyone around us. "Please raise your glass and repeat loudly the six words we can now say without a hint of uncertainty."

"Welcome Zelda Malia Lynn Regenbogen Barnz."

Everyone repeats the words, glasses held high.

28

You are just over one and take your first steps toward us in the Griffith Park playground. Aba screams with delight and I surprise myself by bursting into tears. I am my father's son.

A birthday card arrives a few days later:

> Hey Kiddo,
>
> Sorry it has been a while since I have seen you. I plan to be with you soon. I really wish I could have been there for your first birthday but I just got a new job a couple of weeks ago and don't have the money. I feel kind of bad I missed this because I had been thinking about it for months. Life doesn't always go as you planned. That is the number one thing I've learned from all of this. You just do what you can with what you've got. Anyway, on your first birthday I wish you a peaceful heart and a strong mind. I'm sure you already have that since

you're half my blood. I also want you to know that I don't understand what your mother has done or the California judicial system but I forgive them both and I only wish you can have a joyful life regardless. I know in my heart that Ben and Dan will love and care for you and that's enough to get me by.

I miss you. I love you. With love from your father, Liam

We put the card away in a box that we will share with Zelda when she is older.

～

What will it be like for you to read this? Will you fault us for what we did? Will you understand why?

～

Four months later, almost a year after the depositions, Liam calls the house. I am at a gym class with Zelda. Liam asks after Zelda and tells Daniel that he is writing poetry.

～

Zelda is almost two. We haven't heard from Liam in a year, but we speak with Emma every few months. I want to keep in touch with her. She holds a place in my heart forever. I also want to know where she is if Zelda chooses to meet her.

～

You are just over two and Ana has brought you to Good Samaritan Hospital to meet your brother, Dashiell. Your voice echoes down the hallway and when I step out to greet you I see you run into another room. Already whip-smart you must have noticed your parents weren't there because you came right back out without missing a beat. You see me and run into my arms. Together we enter the room. You are ecstatic to meet your one-day-old brother. You sit on the bed and insist on holding him in your arms.

～

Sometime after Zelda's second birthday, a letter arrives from Liam's sister:

> Dear Ben and Daniel:
>
> I am writing to say that I hope you can be a part of our family. I know that until she is old enough to understand that you are her parents and Liam is her father you may be uncomfortable with that idea. My brother has told me that you are both very nice gentlemen and by the photos I can tell she is very loved and healthy. I can empathize with the feelings you must have had going through this whole ordeal and know that I would have done what I could to keep her if I were in your position. I guess at first I was upset at the whole situation, but after giving birth to my own daughter and becoming a mother I realized that adopting a child is no different. There is still the attachment and love regardless of biology. For now, I choose to look at the two of you as friends and when you are ready, I welcome you to our family with open arms. I wish you both well.
>
> Take Care, Melissa

We add this note to Zelda's box.

∼

You are three and feverish. We are in New York City, staying at my parents' brownstone for the Christmas holiday. I am holding you in my arms when you push yourself off my chest and proceed to throw up all over me (a story you will love retelling your friends).

∼

You are four and dash off paintings of rainbows, one after the other. You are five and bake psychedelic fairy cakes, which you leave on our balcony at night so the 'fairies have something to eat.' You are six and climb over rocks in Mexico with your cousins in search of crabs while the waves crash around you. You are seven and your teacher declares you 'an old soul.'

∼

You are eight and in First Grade and have a school assignment to make a clothespin doll, representing your cultural heritage. We give you the choice: you could honor your Russian Regenbogen side, or your biological Irish ancestry side, or both.

You choose Regenbogen.

~

You are nine and declare that you want to take Latin lessons.

~

You are ten. Double digits. 'Two hands,' you like to point out. You have started to write poems.

> I am from the beautiful flow of the river, lapping on dry ground and turning it wet.
>
> And from the ripple of water as I skip stones across the surface.
>
> I am from the babbling brook as its water laps against stone
>
> And from the slurping sound of animals drinking.
>
> I am from the cool salty water as my brother splashes me in the face
>
> And from the delicious picnic my family brought.
>
> I am from the dense, wet marsh as my shoes start to sink into the wet banks.
>
> And from the chilly, frosty water as I reach my hand down into the river.
>
> I am from the pleasant smell of the rich plants growing near the banks
>
> And from the pure, refreshing scent of the cool waters.
>
> I am from sadness of the thrashed rivers,
>
> And from happiness of the beauty in nature.

- Zelda Barnz; Spring 2011

~

ben barnz

You are ten and I am researching and writing this book. I Facebook Emma and ask if she might share some thoughts on the experience. Three days later I receive an email:

Hello! I got your Facebook message and decided to respond in an email instead of on there because I had a feeling it may be a loooooong message. LOL.

This may sound unbelievable but overall the experience was wonderful. You guys couldn't have been more giving & patient with me even when I was having a bitchy day & didn't feel like going anywhere. This brings me to the only regrets I have. I do regret not being more grateful while I was in California. You guys took such amazing care or me & I was (to put it lightly) a huge brat at times. I try to tell myself that it's because I just felt like a big oompa loompa in a world where everybody is perfect but that is no excuse & my mother would smack me upside the head if she knew what a jerk I was at times.

I even look back at Zelda's birth & smile. It all went so smoothly & it was all because of the great deal of planning you guys had done. We sailed right in with no waiting or huge amounts of paperwork & they made sure I had barely any discomfort at all. Us three just hung out & played Phase 10 until it was time. I do wish I had let you guys be in the room to see your first-born be born. That is the one & only thing I would change about that day.

I'm not sure if the whole after-the-fact court drama qualifies as a regret (with the exception of how much time & money it cost you guys). Sure things would have gone a lot smoother for everybody if that idiot Liam wouldn't have pulled that shit after Zelda was born but I feel like it brought us all even closer together & made me realize, once again, that I had made the very best decision & would fight to keep Zelda where she belongs. Remember the "baby lawyer" cried at the end when we won & we decided that it was probably a rare occurrence?

I can't believe it's been 10 YEARS! Time really goes by fast. My sister & I went to buy flowers to plant for our mom a while back & when we walked into one of the areas I got a whiff of something that smells exactly how I remember LA smelling. I even said out loud "Oooh something in here smells like California did." I'm pretty sure my sister thinks I'm nuts but that happens a lot. Same thing happens anytime I smell a minty soap. You guys had set up my apartment with a bunch of yummy soaps & things & I have been looking for the seaweed/mint/ I don't know body wash since I've been back. My time there couldn't have been better & it's all because of you and Daniel bending over backwards for me every single day. I have never for one second regretted my decision but if I ever did, I could rest easy knowing Zelda is with two of the most loving people on the planet.

I will wrap up this "note" with the hardest question. What shoots through my mind when I see a picture of Zelda...Soooo many things. I'm (of course) thrilled to see that everything is exactly how I had imagined it would be the first time I spoke with you. She is so beautiful & gets to see so many different places & meet so many amazing people. And she has a little brother!! I have to admit I'm a little jealous of that haha. I always wanted a brother. I can't help but feel very proud of myself for finding you guys. It was obviously meant to be & I can't imagine my life without you & Daniel in it. We all helped each other in different ways & I am so happy with the way everything has turned out. I love you all & hope you are all happy & well.

xoxo

Emma

~

I love you so much it hurts sometimes. I wonder if that ever goes away. I should ask my parents.

~

You are twelve and today is the first day at your new school. You walk onto the campus without even a glance over your shoulder. I am filled with pride. This is the point. This is what I want for you, to be independent. Still, it hurts.

∾

You are thirteen and statuesque and smart and taller than I am.

∾

You are fourteen. At night, I continue my bedtime routine. I can't sleep without it. First, I sneak into your brother's room, kiss the palm of my hand and hold it above his sleeping head. "You are enough. You are worthwhile." My hand then rests above his chest, "I wish you an open heart." Then I guide my hand over the length of his body and kiss his head.

Then I walk into your room. I hold my hand over you and say the same words to you. "You are enough. You are worthwhile." Just before I leave your room I turn and whisper: "I love you."

Because I always end this way.

"I love you."

Then I close the door.

acknowledgements

I have been writing this memoir—on and off—for the last ten years. During that time I have raised children, produced movies, manufactured diaper bags, baked desserts for George Lucas's wedding and written when and where I could. The process has been gloriously circuitous. How can I begin to thank everyone who helped me along the way?

First and foremost, I must thank our birthparents—especially our birthmothers. You are my heroes in the truest sense of the word. You each bestowed a gift that is nothing short of a life-defining miracle. I cannot begin to express the depths of my gratitude.

I have changed names to protect people's privacy but they know who they are:

My deepest appreciation to our lawyer "Jonathan"—you are indeed a glorious builder of bridges. To our gynecologist "Dr. Davis"—we want you to know that we fantasized about adopting a third child just so we could go through it all with you again. "Nicole"—your guidance, determination and belief in the law kept us rooted even when it felt like the smallest wind might blow us away. "Scott"—you are the very definition of the kindness of strangers. And "Liam"—I know this experience was complicated and difficult for you, but I am now and always thankful to you for the gift of our daughter.

To all of our friends and family members who stood arm and arm with us and reassured us and loved us in our darkest moments—thanks and thanks and more thanks.

Kevin O'Connor—my kind, intelligent, steadfast agent—you said "yes" and I am eternally grateful to you. Nancy Cleary and everyone at Wyatt-MacKenzie—you too said "yes," forcefully, whole-heartedly and passionately—I am deeply thankful to you. And Jess Cagle—yet another brilliant and generous stranger—who read We and saw me; but more importantly saw all the me's and we's that have come before—and those that will come after—thank you.

To all the people who read early drafts, to the Ucross Foundation for offering me a residency and a cabin of my own, to anyone and everyone who encouraged me, pushed me and marched alongside with me—thank you.

And of course my folks for showing me how to parent, for growing with me and for teaching me how to love and forgive.

My children...my children...one day you will understand the depth of my love. You are my heart.

Finally, Daniel, my love— how do I begin to thank you? You are my partner in every sense of the word. That I get to travel through this miraculous, bumpy, exhausting, exhilarating life with you is beyond any teenage fantasy of what love might be. There is not a single word, nor a million, that could express how I feel about you.